MznLnx

Missing Links Exam Preps

Exam Prep for

College Algebra

Coburn, 1st Edition

The MznLnx Exam Prep is your link from the texbook and lecture to your exams.
The MznLnx Exam Preps are unauthorized and comprehensive reviews of your textbooks.

All material provided by MznLnx and Rico Publications (c) 2010
Textbook publishers and textbook authors do not particpate in or contribute to these reviews.

MznLnx

Rico
Publications

Exam Prep for College Algebra
1st Edition
Coburn

Publisher: Raymond Houge
Assistant Editor: Michael Rouger
Text and Cover Designer: Lisa Buckner
Marketing Manager: Sara Swagger
Project Manager, Editorial Production: Jerry Emerson
Art Director: Vernon Lowerui

Product Manager: Dave Mason
Editorial Assitant: Rachel Guzmanji
Pedagogy: Debra Long
Cover Image: Jim Reed/Getty Images
Text and Cover Printer: City Printing, Inc.
Compositor: Media Mix, Inc.

(c) 2010 Rico Publications

ALL RIGHTS RESERVED. No part of this work covered by the copyright may be reproduced or used in any form or by an means--graphic, electronic, or mechanical, including photocopying, recording, taping, Web distribution, information storage, and retrieval systems, or in any other manner--without the written permission of the publisher.

Printed in the United States
ISBN:

For more information about our products, contact us at:

Dave.Mason@RicoPublications.com

For permission to use material from this text or

product, submit a request online to:

Dave.Mason@RicoPublications.com

Contents

CHAPTER 1
Equations and Inequalities 1

CHAPTER 2
Functions and Graphs 38

CHAPTER 3
Operations on Functions and Analyzing Graphs 58

CHAPTER 4
Polynomial and Rational Functions 78

CHAPTER 5
Exponential and Logarithmic Functions 92

CHAPTER 6
Systems of Equations and Inequalities 105

CHAPTER 7
Conic Sections and Non-Linear Systems 122

CHAPTER 8
Additional Topics in Algebra 131

ANSWER KEY 144

TO THE STUDENT

COMPREHENSIVE

The *MznLnx* Exam Prep series is designed to help you pass your exams. Editors at MznLnx review your textbooks and then prepare these practice exams to help you master the textbook material. Unlike study guides, workbooks, and practice tests provided by the texbook publisher and textbook authors, *MznLnx* gives you **all** of the material in each chapter in exam form, not just samples, so you can be sure to nail your exam.

MECHANICAL

The MznLnx Exam Prep series creates exams that will help you learn the subject matter as well as test you on your understanding. Each question is designed to help you master the concept. Just working through the exams, you gain an understanding of the subject--its a simple mechanical process that produces success.

INTEGRATED STUDY GUIDE AND REVIEW

MznLnx is not just a set of exams designed to test you, its also a comprehensive review of the subject content. Each exam question is also a review of the concept, making sure that you will get the answer correct without having to go to other sources of material. You learn as you go! Its the easiest way to pass an exam.

HUMOR

Studying can be tedious and dry. MznLnx's instructional design includes moderate humor within the exam questions on occassion, to break the tedium and revitalize the brain

Chapter 1. Equations and Inequalities

1. _____ is the estimation of a physical quantity such as distance, energy, temperature, or time.
   a. Thing
   b. Measurement1
   c. Undefined
   d. Undefined

2. In mathematics a _____ is a function which defines a distance between elements of a set.
   a. Metric2
   b. Thing
   c. Undefined
   d. Undefined

3. The _____ is a decimalized system of measurement based on the metre and the gram.
   a. Concept
   b. Metric System3
   c. Undefined
   d. Undefined

4. The _____ of measurement are a globally standardized and modernized form of the metric system.
   a. Units4
   b. Thing
   c. Undefined
   d. Undefined

5. In mathematics, the _____ , or members of a set or more generally a class are all those objects which when collected together make up the set or class.
   a. Elements5
   b. Thing
   c. Undefined
   d. Undefined

6. In mathematics, a _____ can mean either an element of the set {1, 2, 3, ...} (i.e the positive integers or the counting numbers) or an element of the set {0, 1, 2, 3, ...} (i.e. the non-negative integers).

a. Thing
b. Natural number6
c. Undefined
d. Undefined

7. In measure theory, a _____ is a set that is negligible for the purposes of the measure in question.
a. Null set7
b. Concept
c. Undefined
d. Undefined

8. In mathematics, a _____ can be thought of as any collection of distinct objects considered as a whole.
a. Set8
b. Thing
c. Undefined
d. Undefined

9. _____ is a mathematical notation for describing a set by stating the properties that its members must satisfy.
a. Thing
b. Set-builder notation9
c. Undefined
d. Undefined

10. _____ are groups whose members are members of another set or a set contained within another set.
a. Thing
b. Subsets10
c. Undefined
d. Undefined

11. In mathematics, a _____ can mean either an element of the set {1, 2, 3, ...} (i.e the positive integers) or an element of the set {0, 1, 2, 3, ...} (i.e. the non-negative integers).

a. Whole number11
b. Concept
c. Undefined
d. Undefined

12. _____ are the basic objects of study in graph theory. Informally speaking, a graph is a set of objects called points, nodes, or vertices connected by links called lines or edges.
   a. Graphs12
   b. Thing
   c. Undefined
   d. Undefined

13. Mathematical _____ is used in mathematics, and throughout the physical sciences, engineering, and economics. The complexity of such _____ ranges from relatively simple symbolic representations, such as numbers 1 and 2; function symbols sin and +, to conceptual symbols, such as lim and dy/dx; to equations and variables.
   a. Notation13
   b. Thing
   c. Undefined
   d. Undefined

14. A _____ is a mathematical concept used to describe and assess quantity. It is an abstract entity representing a quantity, used to express how many are being referred to, or how much there is of some thing or property.
   a. Thing
   b. Number14
   c. Undefined
   d. Undefined

15. A _____ is a set of numbers that designate location in a given reference system, such as x,y in a planar _____ system or an x,y,z in a three-dimensional _____ system.
   a. Thing
   b. Coordinate15
   c. Undefined
   d. Undefined

Chapter 1. Equations and Inequalities

16. The _____ are the only integral domain whose positive elements are well-ordered, and in which order is preserved by addition. Like the natural numbers, the _____ form a countably infinite set. The set of all _____ is usually denoted in mathematics by a boldface Z .
   a. Integers16
   b. Thing
   c. Undefined
   d. Undefined

17. A _____ is a number that is less than zero.
   a. Negative number17
   b. Thing
   c. Undefined
   d. Undefined

18. A _____ is a one-dimensional picture in which the integers are shown as specially-marked points evenly spaced on a line.
   a. Number line18
   b. Thing
   c. Undefined
   d. Undefined

19. In mathematics, a _____ number is a number which can be expressed as a ratio of two integers. Non-integer _____ numbers (commonly called fractions) are usually written as the vulgar fraction a / b, where b is not zero.
   a. Rational19
   b. Thing
   c. Undefined
   d. Undefined

20. In mathematics, a _____ is a number which can be expressed as a ratio of two integers. Non-integer rational numbers (commonly called fractions) are usually written as the vulgar fraction a / b, where b is not zero.
   a. Concept
   b. Rational number20
   c. Undefined
   d. Undefined

Chapter 1. Equations and Inequalities

21. A _____ is the part of a fraction that tells how many equal parts make up a whole, and which is used in the name of the fraction: "halves", "thirds", "fourths" or "quarters", "fifths" and so on.
    a. Denominator21
    b. Concept
    c. Undefined
    d. Undefined

22. A _____ can be described as an infinitely thin, infinitely long, perfectly straight curve containing an infinite number of points.
    a. Line22
    b. Thing
    c. Undefined
    d. Undefined

23. The _____ of a mathematical object is its size: a property by which it can be larger or smaller than other objects of the same kind; in technical terms, an ordering of the class of objects to which it belongs.
    a. Thing
    b. Magnitude23
    c. Undefined
    d. Undefined

24. The _____ numeral system has ten as its base. It is the most widely used numeral system, perhaps because humans have four fingers and a thumb on each hand, giving a total of ten digits over both hands.
    a. Thing
    b. Decimal24
    c. Undefined
    d. Undefined

25. In linear algebra, Gauss–Jordan elimination is a version of Gaussian elimination that puts zeros both above and below each pivot element as it goes from the top row of the given matrix to the bottom. In other words, _____ elimination brings a matrix to reduced row echelon form, whereas Gaussian elimination takes it only as far as row echelon form.
    a. Thing
    b. Gauss-Jordan25
    c. Undefined
    d. Undefined

26. _____ is a version of Gaussian elimination that puts zeros both above and below each pivot element as it goes from the top row of the given matrix to the bottom.
   a. Thing
   b. Gauss-Jordan elimination26
   c. Undefined
   d. Undefined

27. _____ is an algorithm which can be used to determine the solutions of a system of linear equations, to find the rank of a matrix, and to calculate the inverse of an invertible square matrix.
   a. Gaussian elimination27
   b. Thing
   c. Undefined
   d. Undefined

28. In mathematics, an _____ number is any real number that is not a rational number- that is, it is a number which cannot be expressed as a fraction m/n, where m and n are integers.
   a. Thing
   b. Irrational28
   c. Undefined
   d. Undefined

29. In mathematics, _____ are any real number that is not a rational number ¡ª that is, it is a number which cannot be expressed as m/n, where m and n are integers.
   a. Thing
   b. Irrational numbers29
   c. Undefined
   d. Undefined

30. A _____ decimal is a decimal for which there is no digit to the right of the decimal point, as all digits farther from the right are zero.
   a. Thing
   b. Nonterminating30
   c. Undefined
   d. Undefined

Chapter 1. Equations and Inequalities

31. A _____ signifies a point or points of probability on a subject e.g., the _____ of creativity, which allows for the formation of rule or norm or law by interpretation of the phenomena events that can be created.
    a. Principle31
    b. Thing
    c. Undefined
    d. Undefined

32. In mathematics, a _____ may be described informally as a number that can be given by an infinite decimal representation.
    a. Real number32
    b. Thing
    c. Undefined
    d. Undefined

33. In mathematics, a matrix is in _____ form, also known as row canonical form - the resulting matrix is sometimes called a Hermite matrix; if it satisfies the following requirements: All nonzero rows are above any rows of all zeroes, The leading coefficient of a row is always to the right of the leading coefficient of the row above it, All leading coefficients are 1, and All entries above a leading coefficient in the same column are zero.
    a. Reduced row-echelon33
    b. Thing
    c. Undefined
    d. Undefined

34. In mathematics, a matrix is in _____ if is satisfies the following requirements. All nonzero rows are above any rows of all zeroes. The leading coefficient of a row is always strictly to the right of the leading coefficient of the row above it.
    a. Row-echelon form34
    b. Thing
    c. Undefined
    d. Undefined

35. In plane geometry, a _____ is a polygon with four equal sides, four right angles, and parallel opposite sides. In algebra, the _____ of a number is that number multiplied by itself.
    a. Square35
    b. Thing
    c. Undefined
    d. Undefined

Chapter 1. Equations and Inequalities

36. In mathematics, a _____ of a number x is a number r such that r^2 = x, or in words, a number r whose square (the result of multiplying the number by itself) is x.
   a. Square root36
   b. Thing
   c. Undefined
   d. Undefined

37. A _____ decimal is a decimal fraction which ends after a definite number of digits.
   a. Terminating37
   b. Thing
   c. Undefined
   d. Undefined

38. _____ represent rational numbers whose fractions in lowest terms are of the form $k/(2^n 5^m)$.
   a. Thing
   b. Terminating decimals38
   c. Undefined
   d. Undefined

39. In mathematics, a _____ of a complex-valued function f is a member x of the domain of f such that f(x) vanishes at x, that is, x : f (x) = 0.
   a. Thing
   b. Root39
   c. Undefined
   d. Undefined

40. In linear algebra, a _____ or minor of a matrix A is the determinant of some smaller square matrix, cut down from A.
   a. Cofactor40
   b. Thing
   c. Undefined
   d. Undefined

41. In mathematics, an inequality is a statement about the relative size or order of two objects. For example 14 > 10, or 14 is _____ 10.

a. Thing
b. Greater than41
c. Undefined
d. Undefined

42. In mathematics, an inequality is a statement about the relative size or order of two objects. For example 9 < 10, or 9 is _____ 10.
a. Less than42
b. Thing
c. Undefined
d. Undefined

43. A _____ is a symbolic representation denoting a quantity or expression. It often represents an "unknown" quantity that has the potential to change.
a. Thing
b. Variable43
c. Undefined
d. Undefined

44. In mathematics, an _____ is a statement about the relative size or order of two objects.
a. Thing
b. Inequality44
c. Undefined
d. Undefined

45. In mathematics, a _____ is a rectangular table of numbers or, more generally, a table consisting of abstract quantities that can be added and multiplied.
a. Thing
b. Matrix45
c. Undefined
d. Undefined

46. In philosophy, mathematics, and logic, a _____ is an attribute of an object; thus a red object is said to have the _____ of redness.

a. Property46
b. Thing
c. Undefined
d. Undefined

47. _____ are objects, characters, or other concrete representations of ideas, concepts, or other abstractions.
a. Symbols47
b. Thing
c. Undefined
d. Undefined

48. In mathematics, the _____ (or modulus) of a real number is its numerical value without regard to its sign.
a. Thing
b. Absolute value48
c. Undefined
d. Undefined

49. In Euclidean geometry, a _____ is the set of all points in a plane at a fixed distance, called the radius, from a given point, the center.
a. Circle49
b. Thing
c. Undefined
d. Undefined

50. In mathematics, an _____ .
a. Thing
b. Ellipse50
c. Undefined
d. Undefined

51. In geometry, an _____ is a point at which a line segment or ray terminates.

Chapter 1. Equations and Inequalities

   a. Endpoint51
   b. Thing
   c. Undefined
   d. Undefined

52. In mathematics, a _____ is a type of conic section defined as the intersection between a right circular conical surface and a plane which cuts through both halves of the cone.
   a. Thing
   b. Hyperbola52
   c. Undefined
   d. Undefined

53. In mathematics, the _____ is a conic section generated by the intersection of a right circular conical surface and a plane parallel to a generating straight line of that surface. It can also be defined as locus of points in a plane which are equidistant from a given point.
   a. Thing
   b. Parabola53
   c. Undefined
   d. Undefined

54. In mathematics, a _____ section is a curve that can be formed by intersecting a cone with a plane.
   a. Conic54
   b. Thing
   c. Undefined
   d. Undefined

55. An _____ is a mathematical statement, in symbols, that two things are the same or equivalent. Equations are written with an equal sign, as in 2 + 3 = 5.
   a. Thing
   b. Equation55
   c. Undefined
   d. Undefined

56. _____ commonly refers to the 'output' of a function.

a. Thing
b. Value56
c. Undefined
d. Undefined

57. In arithmetic, the _____ refers to the number b in an expression of the form b^n.
a. Thing
b. Base57
c. Undefined
d. Undefined

58. In mathematics, _____ growth occurs when the growth rate of a function is always proportional to the function's current size.
a. Exponential58
b. Thing
c. Undefined
d. Undefined

59. _____ is a notation for writing numbers that is often used by scientists and mathematicians to make it easier to write large and small numbers.
a. Scientific notation59
b. Thing
c. Undefined
d. Undefined

60. _____ is a mathematical operation, written a^n, involving two numbers, the base a and the exponent n.
a. Thing
b. Exponentiating60
c. Undefined
d. Undefined

61. _____ is both a number and a numerical digit used to represent that number in numerals. As a number, it means nothing — an absence of other values.

a. Zero61
b. Thing
c. Undefined
d. Undefined

62. In mathematics, especially in elementary arithmetic, _____ is an arithmetic operation which is the inverse of multiplication.
a. Division62
b. Thing
c. Undefined
d. Undefined

63. The word _____ is used in a variety of ways in mathematics.
a. Thing
b. Index63
c. Undefined
d. Undefined

64. A _____ is a number which is the cube of an integer.
a. Thing
b. Perfect cube64
c. Undefined
d. Undefined

65. The term _____ can refer to an integer which is the square of some other integer, or an algebraic expression that can be factored as the square of some other expression.
a. Perfect square65
b. Thing
c. Undefined
d. Undefined

66. In mathematics, _____ are used to indicate the square root of a number.

a. Thing
   b. Radicals66
   c. Undefined
   d. Undefined

67. The _____ is the number or expression underneath the radical sign.
   a. Radicand67
   b. Thing
   c. Undefined
   d. Undefined

68. A _____ of a number is a number a such that $a^3 = x$.
   a. Thing
   b. Cube root68
   c. Undefined
   d. Undefined

69. _____ are of a number n in its third power-the result of multiplying it by itself three times.
   a. Cubes69
   b. Thing
   c. Undefined
   d. Undefined

70. In arithmetic and algebra, when a number or expression is both preceded and followed by a binary operation, an _____ is required for which operation should be applied first.
   a. Thing
   b. Order of operations70
   c. Undefined
   d. Undefined

71. In geometry, a _____ (Greek words diairo = divide and metro = measure) of a circle is any straight line segment that passes through the centre and whose endpoints are on the circular boundary, or, in more modern usage, the length of such a line segment. When using the word in the more modern sense, one speaks of the _____ rather than a _____, because all diameters of a circle have the same length. This length is twice the radius. The _____ of a circle is also the longest chord that the circle has.

a. Diameter71
b. Thing
c. Undefined
d. Undefined

72. In mathematics, a _____ is a constant multiplicative factor of a certain object. The object can be such things as a variable, a vector, a function, etc. For example, the _____ of $9x^2$ is 9.
   a. Coefficient72
   b. Thing
   c. Undefined
   d. Undefined

73. In mathematics and the mathematical sciences, a _____ is a fixed, but possibly unspecified, value. This is in contrast to a variable, which is not fixed.
   a. Constant73
   b. Thing
   c. Undefined
   d. Undefined

74. _____ is a fixed, but possibly unspecified, value. This is in contrast to a variable, which is not fixed.
   a. Constant term74
   b. Thing
   c. Undefined
   d. Undefined

75. _____ is a branch of mathematics concerning the study of structure, relation and quantity.
   a. Concept
   b. Algebra75
   c. Undefined
   d. Undefined

76. A _____ is any value or expression separated from another _____ by a + or - sign in an overall expression.

Chapter 1. Equations and Inequalities

a. Thing
b. Term76
c. Undefined
d. Undefined

77. An _____ is a combination of numbers, operators, grouping symbols and/or free variables and bound variables arranged in a meaningful way which can be evaluated..
a. Thing
b. Expression77
c. Undefined
d. Undefined

78. A _____ is an abstract model that uses mathematical language to describe the behavior of a system. Eykhoff defined a _____ as 'a representation of the essential aspects of an existing system which presents knowledge of that system in usable form'.
a. Thing
b. Mathematical model78
c. Undefined
d. Undefined

79. In Euclidean geometry, a _____ is moving every point a constant distance in a specified direction.
a. Concept
b. Translation79
c. Undefined
d. Undefined

80. _____ is the mathematical operation of combining or adding two numbers to obtain an equal simple amount or total.
a. Addition80
b. Thing
c. Undefined
d. Undefined

81. The _____ is a property of multiplication or addition where the product or sum remains the same, regardless of whether or not the order of the addends or factors are changed.

a. Thing
b. Commutative property81
c. Undefined
d. Undefined

82. In mathematics, _____ is an elementary arithmetic operation. When one of the numbers is a whole number, _____ is the repeated sum of the other number.
a. Multiplication82
b. Thing
c. Undefined
d. Undefined

83. In mathematics, the _____ inverse, or opposite, of a number n is the number that, when added to n, yields zero. The _____ inverse of n is denoted −n.
a. Thing
b. Additive83
c. Undefined
d. Undefined

84. In mathematics the _____ of a set which is equipped with the operation of addition is an element which, when added to any other element x in the set, yields x.
a. Concept
b. Additive identity84
c. Undefined
d. Undefined

85. In mathematics, the _____ of a number n is the number that, when added to n, yields zero. The _____ of n is denoted −n. For example, 7 is −7, because 7 + (−7) = 0, and the _____ of −0.3 is 0.3, because −0.3 + 0.3 = 0.
a. Additive inverse85
b. Thing
c. Undefined
d. Undefined

86. An _____ is an equality that remains true regardless of the values of any variables that appear within it, to distinguish it from an equality which is true under more particular conditions.

Chapter 1. Equations and Inequalities

   a. Thing
   b. Identity86
   c. Undefined
   d. Undefined

87. In mathematics, an _____ (or neutral element) is a special type of element of a set with respect to a binary operation on that set.
   a. Concept
   b. Identity element87
   c. Undefined
   d. Undefined

88. _____ element of an element x with respect to a binary operation * with identity element e is an element y such that x * y = y * x = e. In particular,
   a. Thing
   b. Inverse88
   c. Undefined
   d. Undefined

89. In mathematics, the idea of _____ generalises the concepts of negation, in relation to addition, and reciprocal, in relation to multiplication.
   a. Thing
   b. Inverse element89
   c. Undefined
   d. Undefined

90. In mathematics, the _____ inverse of a number x, denoted $1/x$ or x^{-1}, is the number which, when multiplied by x, yields 1. The _____ inverse of x is also called the reciprocal of x.
   a. Thing
   b. Multiplicative90
   c. Undefined
   d. Undefined

91. In mathematics, the _____ of a number x, denoted $1/x$ or x^{-1}, is the number which, when multiplied by x, yields 1. The _____ of x is also called the reciprocal of x.

Chapter 1. Equations and Inequalities 19

   a. Thing
   b. Multiplicative inverse91
   c. Undefined
   d. Undefined

92. In mathematics, the additive inverse, or _____ of a number n is the number that, when added to n, yields zero. The additive inverse of n is denoted −n. For example, 7 is −7, because 7 + (−7) = 0, and the additive inverse of −0.3 is 0.3, because −0.3 + 0.3 = 0.
   a. Opposite92
   b. Thing
   c. Undefined
   d. Undefined

93. In mathematics, the multiplicative inverse of a number x, denoted 1/x or x^{-1}, is the number which, when multiplied by x, yields 1. The multiplicative inverse of x is also called the _____ of x.
   a. Thing
   b. Reciprocal93
   c. Undefined
   d. Undefined

94. In mathematics, _____ is a property that a binary operation can have. Within an expression containing two or more of the same associative operators in a row, the order of operations does not matter as long as the sequence of the operands is not changed.
   a. Associativity94
   b. Thing
   c. Undefined
   d. Undefined

95. In mathematics, and in particular in abstract algebra, the _____ is a property of binary operations that generalises the distributive law from elementary algebra.
   a. Distributive property95
   b. Thing
   c. Undefined
   d. Undefined

96. _____ is the force per unit area applied on a surface in a direction perpendicular to that surface.

a. Thing
b. Pressure96
c. Undefined
d. Undefined

97. In mathematics and in the sciences, a _____ is a concise way of expressing information symbolically or a general relationship between quantities.
a. Thing
b. Formula97
c. Undefined
d. Undefined

98. The _____ of a solid object is the three-dimensional concept of how much space it occupies, often quantified numerically.
a. Volume98
b. Thing
c. Undefined
d. Undefined

99. _____ is a geometric arrangement of the binomial coefficients in a triangle. It is named after Blaise Pascal in the English-speaking world, even though others studied it centuries before him in Persia, China, India, and Italy.
a. Thing
b. Pascal's triangle99
c. Undefined
d. Undefined

100. In mathematics, a _____ is the result of multiplying, or an expression that identifies factors to be multiplied.
a. Product100
b. Thing
c. Undefined
d. Undefined

101. A _____ is one of the basic shapes of geometry: a polygon with three vertices and three sides which are straight line segments.

Chapter 1. Equations and Inequalities

a. Triangle101
b. Thing
c. Undefined
d. Undefined

102. _____ has many meanings, most of which simply .
a. Thing
b. Power102
c. Undefined
d. Undefined

103. In mathematics, a _____ is the end result of a division problem. It can also be expressed as the number of times the divisor divides into the dividend.
a. Thing
b. Quotient103
c. Undefined
d. Undefined

104. In mathematics, there are several meanings of _____ depending on the subject.
a. Thing
b. Degree104
c. Undefined
d. Undefined

105. In mathematics, a _____ is a particular kind of polynomial, having just one term.
a. Monomial105
b. Thing
c. Undefined
d. Undefined

106. In mathematics, a _____ is an expression that is constructed from one or more variables and constants, using only the operations of addition, subtraction, multiplication, and constant positive whole number exponents. is a _____. Note in particular that division by an expression containing a variable is not in general allowed in polynomials.

a. Polynomial106
b. Thing
c. Undefined
d. Undefined

107. In elementary algebra, a _____ is a polynomial with two terms: the sum of two monomials. It is the simplest kind of polynomial except for a monomial.
a. Thing
b. Binomial107
c. Undefined
d. Undefined

108. A _____ is a polynomial consisting of three terms; in other words, it is the sum of three monomials.
a. Trinomial108
b. Thing
c. Undefined
d. Undefined

109. _____ is one of the four basic arithmetic operations; it is essentially the opposite of addition.
a. Subtraction109
b. Thing
c. Undefined
d. Undefined

110. In algebra, a _____ is a binomial formed by taking the opposite of the second term of a binomial.
a. Thing
b. Conjugate110
c. Undefined
d. Undefined

111. A _____ is a method of using property as security for the payment of a debt.

Chapter 1. Equations and Inequalities

a. Thing
b. Mortgage111
c. Undefined
d. Undefined

112. In mathematics, the _____ divisor of two non-zero integers, is the largest positive integer that divides both numbers without remainder.
a. Thing
b. Greatest common112
c. Undefined
d. Undefined

113. In Math the greates common divisor sometimes known as the _____ of two non- zero integers.
a. Thing
b. Greatest common factor113
c. Undefined
d. Undefined

114. _____ is the largest positive integer that divides both numbers without remainder.
a. Thing
b. Common factor114
c. Undefined
d. Undefined

115. In mathematics, factorization (British English: factorisation) or factoring is the decomposition of an object (for example, a number, a polynomial, or a matrix) into a product of other objects, or _____, which when multiplied together give the original
a. Factors115
b. Thing
c. Undefined
d. Undefined

116. In abstract algebra, _____ consists of sets with binary operations that satisfy certain axioms.

Chapter 1. Equations and Inequalities

   a. Grouping116
   b. Thing
   c. Undefined
   d. Undefined

117. In mathematics, _____ is the decomposition of an object into a product of other objects, or factors, which when multiplied together give the original.
   a. Factoring117
   b. Thing
   c. Undefined
   d. Undefined

118. In mathematics, a _____ number (or a _____) is a natural number that has exactly two (distinct) natural number divisors, which are 1 and the _____ number itself.
   a. Thing
   b. Prime118
   c. Undefined
   d. Undefined

119. A _____ is the result of the addition of a set of numbers. The numbers may be natural numbers, complex numbers, matrices, or still more complicated objects. An infinite _____ is a subtle procedure known as a series.
   a. Sum119
   b. Thing
   c. Undefined
   d. Undefined

120. In mathematics, a _____ is a homogeneous polynomial of degree two in a number of variables.
   a. Thing
   b. Quadratic form120
   c. Undefined
   d. Undefined

121. In mathematics, a _____ is a quadric surface, with the following equation in Cartesian coordinates: $(x/_a)^2 + (y/_b)^2 = 1$.

Chapter 1. Equations and Inequalities

a. Thing
b. Cylinder121
c. Undefined
d. Undefined

122. _____ is one of the gas laws. It states that: " For a fixed mass of ideal gas at fixed temperature, the product of pressure and volume is a constant. "
a. Thing
b. Boyle's law122
c. Undefined
d. Undefined

123. _____ is the physical law concerning the voluminal laminar stationary flow Φ of incompressible uniform viscous liquid through a cylindrical tude with a constant circular cross-section, experimentally derived in 1838.
a. Poiseuille's law123
b. Thing
c. Undefined
d. Undefined

124. In mathematics, a _____ in elementary terms is any of a variety of different functions from geometry, such as rotations, reflections and translations.
a. Transformation124
b. Thing
c. Undefined
d. Undefined

125. _____ is a gas law
a. Charles's law125
b. Thing
c. Undefined
d. Undefined

126. The _____ are a set of laws that describe the relationship between thermodynamic temperature T, pressure P and volume V of gases.

a. Gas law126
b. Thing
c. Undefined
d. Undefined

127. In mathematics, _____ refers to the rewriting of an expression into a simpler form.
a. Reduction127
b. Thing
c. Undefined
d. Undefined

128. In mathematics, a _____ is a way of expressing a number of equal parts. A _____ consists of two numbers, a numerator which gives the number of equal parts and a denominator which gives the number of those parts that make up a whole.
a. Thing
b. Fraction128
c. Undefined
d. Undefined

129. _____ interest refers to the fact that whenever interest is calculated, it is based not only on the original principal, but also on any unpaid interest that has been added to the principal.
a. Thing
b. Compound129
c. Undefined
d. Undefined

130. In linear algebra, a _____ of a matrix A is the determinant of some smaller square matrix, cut down from A.
a. Thing
b. Minor130
c. Undefined
d. Undefined

131. In mathematics, _____ expressions is used to reduce the expression into the lowest possible term.

Chapter 1. Equations and Inequalities

  a. Simplifying131
  b. Thing
  c. Undefined
  d. Undefined

132. _____ was an Italian physicist, mathematician, astronomer, and philosopher who is closely associated with the scientific revolution.
  a. Person
  b. Galileo Galilei132
  c. Undefined
  d. Undefined

133. _____, or Rationalisation in mathematics is the process of removing a square root or imaginary number from the denominator of a fraction.
  a. Thing
  b. Rationalizing133
  c. Undefined
  d. Undefined

134. The _____ of a right triangle is the triangle's longest side; the side opposite the right angle.
  a. Thing
  b. Hypotenuse134
  c. Undefined
  d. Undefined

135. _____ is a relation in Euclidean geometry among the three sides of a right triangle.
  a. Pythagorean theorem135
  b. Thing
  c. Undefined
  d. Undefined

136. _____ has one 90° internal angle a right angle.

a. Right triangle136
b. Thing
c. Undefined
d. Undefined

137. In mathematics, a _____ is a statement that can be proved on the basis of explicitly stated or previously agreed assumptions.
   a. Theorem137
   b. Thing
   c. Undefined
   d. Undefined

138. A _____ is a numeral used to indicate a count. The most common use of the word today is to name the part of a fraction that tells the number or count of equal parts.
   a. Numerator138
   b. Thing
   c. Undefined
   d. Undefined

139. _____ is the long dimension of any object. The _____ of a thing is the distance between its ends, its linear extent as measured from end to end.
   a. Length139
   b. Thing
   c. Undefined
   d. Undefined

140. Kepler's laws of _____ are his primary contributions to astronomy/astrophysics. Kepler, a German mathematician, studied the observations of the legendarily precise Danish astronomer Tycho Brahe, and found around 1605 that these observations followed three relatively simple mathematical laws.
   a. Thing
   b. Planetary motion140
   c. Undefined
   d. Undefined

141. The word _____ comes from the Latin word linearis, which means created by lines.

a. Linear141
b. Thing
c. Undefined
d. Undefined

142. A _____ is an equation in which each term is either a constant or the product of a constant times the first power of a variable.
   a. Linear equation142
   b. Thing
   c. Undefined
   d. Undefined

143. The _____ of equality is the formal name for the property of equality that allows one to add the same quantity to both sides of an equation.
   a. Concept
   b. Additive property143
   c. Undefined
   d. Undefined

144. Two mathematical objects are equal if and only if they are precisely the same in every way. This defines a binary relation, _____, denoted by the sign of _____ "=" in such a way that the statement "x = y" means that x and y are equal.
   a. Thing
   b. Equality144
   c. Undefined
   d. Undefined

145. The material _____, also known as the material implication or truth functional _____, expresses a property of certain conditionals in logic.
   a. Thing
   b. Conditional145
   c. Undefined
   d. Undefined

146. In logic, a _____ consists of a logical incompatibility between two or more propositions.

Chapter 1. Equations and Inequalities

a. Thing
b. Contradictions146
c. Undefined
d. Undefined

147. The _____ of two integers is the smallest positive integer that is a multiple of both intergers.
a. Thing
b. Least common multiple147
c. Undefined
d. Undefined

148. In mathematics, a _____ is a number, function, or distribution which satisfies an equation.
a. Thing
b. Solution148
c. Undefined
d. Undefined

149. A _____ of a number is the product of that number with any integer.
a. Thing
b. Multiple149
c. Undefined
d. Undefined

150. _____ forms part of thinking. Considered the most complex of all intellectual functions, _____ has been defined as higher-order cognitive process that requires the modulation and control of more routine or fundamental skills.
a. Problem solving150
b. Thing
c. Undefined
d. Undefined

151. _____ means in succession or back-to-back

Chapter 1. Equations and Inequalities

a. Consecutive151
b. Thing
c. Undefined
d. Undefined

152. In chemistry, a _____ is substance made by combining two or more different materials in such a way that no chemical reaction occurs.
a. Mixture152
b. Thing
c. Undefined
d. Undefined

153. _____ is a physical quantity expressing the size of a part of a surface. The term can also be used in a non-mathematical context to be mean "vicinity".
a. Area153
b. Thing
c. Undefined
d. Undefined

154. In mathematics, specifically in topology, a _____ is a two-dimensional manifold. The most familiar examples are those that arise as the boundaries of solid objects in ordinary three-dimensional Euclidean space, E^3.
a. Surface154
b. Thing
c. Undefined
d. Undefined

155. In elementary algebra, an _____ is a set that contains every real number between two indicated numbers and may contain the two numbers themselves.
a. Thing
b. Interval155
c. Undefined
d. Undefined

156. _____ is the notation in which permitted values for a variable are expressed as ranging over a certain interval; "5 < x < 9" is an example of the application of _____.

a. Interval notation156
b. Thing
c. Undefined
d. Undefined

157. A _____ is a set of possible values that a variable can take on in order to satisfy a given set of conditions, which may include equations and inequalities.
   a. Solution set157
   b. Thing
   c. Undefined
   d. Undefined

158. In mathematics, the _____ of two sets A and B is the set that contains all elements of A that also belong to B (or equivalently, all elements of B that also belong to A), but no other elements.
   a. Thing
   b. Intersection158
   c. Undefined
   d. Undefined

159. In set theory and other branches of mathematics, the _____ of a collection of sets is the set that contains everything that belongs to any of the sets, but nothing else.
   a. Union159
   b. Thing
   c. Undefined
   d. Undefined

160. In mathematics, a _____ of a k-place relation $L \subseteq X_1 \times \ldots \times X_k$ is one of the sets X_j, $1 \leq j \leq k$. In the special case where k = 2 and $L \subseteq X_1 \times X_2$ is a function $L : X_1 \to X_2$, it is conventional to refer to X_1 as the _____ of the function and to refer to X_2 as the codomain of the function.
   a. Domain160
   b. Thing
   c. Undefined
   d. Undefined

161. A _____ typically refers to a class of handheld calculators that are capable of plotting graphs, solving equation systems, and performing numerous other tasks with variables.

Chapter 1. Equations and Inequalities

   a. Graphing calculator161
   b. Thing
   c. Undefined
   d. Undefined

162. _____ is a statistical measure of the weight of a person scaled according to height. It was invented between 1830 and 1850 by the Belgian polymath Adolphe Quetelet during the course of developing "social physics".
   a. Body mass index162
   b. Thing
   c. Undefined
   d. Undefined

163. _____ is the ability to hold, receive or absorb, or a measure thereof, similar to the concept of volume.
   a. Capacity163
   b. Concept
   c. Undefined
   d. Undefined

164. _____ is informally a function which satisfies a polynomial equation whose coefficients are themselves polynomials.
   a. Thing
   b. Algebraic function164
   c. Undefined
   d. Undefined

165. In mathematics, a _____ is a polynomial equation of the second degree. The general form is $ax^2 + bx + c = 0$.
   a. Quadratic equation165
   b. Thing
   c. Undefined
   d. Undefined

166. In mathematics, a _____ number is a real or complex number which is not algebraic, that is, not a solution of a non-zero polynomial equation, with rational coefficients.

a. Transcendental166
b. Thing
c. Undefined
d. Undefined

167. The mathematical concept of a _____ expresses the intuitive idea of deterministic dependence between two quantities, one of which is viewed as primary and the other as secondary. A _____ then is a way to associate a unique output for each input of a specified type, for example, a real number or an element of a given set.
a. Thing
b. Function167
c. Undefined
d. Undefined

168. _____ variables are variables other than the independent variable that may bear any effect on the behavior of the subject being studied.
a. Extraneous168
b. Thing
c. Undefined
d. Undefined

169. _____ is a part of mathematics concerned with questions of size, shape, and relative position of figures and with properties of space.
a. Thing
b. Geometry169
c. Undefined
d. Undefined

170. _____ is the path a moving object follows through space.
a. Projectile motion170
b. Thing
c. Undefined
d. Undefined

171. _____ is a business term for the amount of money that a company receives from its activities in a given period, mostly from sales of products and/or services to customers

Chapter 1. Equations and Inequalities

a. Revenue171
b. Thing
c. Undefined
d. Undefined

172. A _____ is a three-dimensional geometric shape formed by straight lines through a fixed point (vertex) to the points of a fixed curve (directrix)
   a. Cone172
   b. Concept
   c. Undefined
   d. Undefined

173. A _____ surface is the surface or face of a solid on its sides. It can also be defined as any face or surface that is not a base.
   a. Lateral173
   b. Thing
   c. Undefined
   d. Undefined

174. In mathematics, an _____ number is a complex number whose square is a negative real number. They were defined in 1572 by Rafael Bombelli.
   a. Imaginary174
   b. Thing
   c. Undefined
   d. Undefined

175. In mathematics, an _____ is a complex number whose square is a negative real number. They were defined in 1572 by Rafael Bombelli.
   a. Thing
   b. Imaginary number175
   c. Undefined
   d. Undefined

176. Leonhard _____ was a pioneering Swiss mathematician and physicist, who spent most of his life in Russia and Germany.

a. Person
b. Euler176
c. Undefined
d. Undefined

177. _____ was a pioneering Swiss mathematician and physicist, who spent most of his life in Russia and Germany
a. Person
b. Euler Leonhard177
c. Undefined
d. Undefined

178. In mathematics, a _____ is a number in the form of a + bi where a and b are real numbers, and i is the imaginary unit, with the property i 2 = −1. The real number a is called the real part of the _____, and the real number b is the imaginary part.
a. Thing
b. Complex number178
c. Undefined
d. Undefined

179. _____ is a technique used in algebra to solve quadratic equations, in analytic geometry for determining the shapes of graphs, and in calculus for computing integrals, including, but hardly limited to, the integrals that define Laplace transforms. The essential objective is to reduce a quadratic polynomial in a variable in an equation or expression to a squared polynomial of linear order. This can reduce an equation or integral to one that is more easily solved or evaluated.
a. Completing the square179
b. Thing
c. Undefined
d. Undefined

180. A quadratic equation with real solutions, called roots, which may be real or complex, is given by the _____: $x = \frac{-b \pm \sqrt{b^2 - 4ac}}{2a}$.
a. Thing
b. Quadratic formula180
c. Undefined
d. Undefined

181. _____ of a polynomial with real or complex coefficients is a certain expression in the coefficients of the polynomial which is equal to zero if and only if the polynomial has a multiple root i.e. a root with multiplicity greater than one in the complex numbers.
   a. Thing
   b. Discriminant181
   c. Undefined
   d. Undefined

182. _____ are any object propelled through space by the application of a force.
   a. Projectiles182
   b. Thing
   c. Undefined
   d. Undefined

183. _____ is the measurement of distance between a specified point and a corresponding plane of reference. If the distance is occupied by a contiguous form of matter, the measurement is colloquially known as how "tall" the form is.
   a. Thing
   b. Height183
   c. Undefined
   d. Undefined

Chapter 2. Functions and Graphs

1. _____ means of or relating to the French philosopher and mathematician René Descartes.
   a. Cartesian1
   b. Thing
   c. Undefined
   d. Undefined

2. In mathematics, the _____ is used to determine each point uniquely in a plane through two numbers, usually called the x-coordinate and the y-coordinate of the point.
   a. Thing
   b. Cartesian coordinate system2
   c. Undefined
   d. Undefined

3. The word _____ comes from the Latin word linearis, which means created by lines.
   a. Thing
   b. Linear3
   c. Undefined
   d. Undefined

4. A _____ is an equation in which each term is either a constant or the product of a constant times the first power of a variable.
   a. Linear equation4
   b. Thing
   c. Undefined
   d. Undefined

5. An _____ is a collection of two not necessarily distinct objects, one of which is distinguished as the first coordinate and the other as the second coordinate.
   a. Ordered pair5
   b. Thing
   c. Undefined
   d. Undefined

6. An _____ is a mathematical statement, in symbols, that two things are the same or equivalent. Equations are written with an equal sign, as in 2 + 3 = 5.

Chapter 2. Functions and Graphs

   a. Thing
   b. Equation6
   c. Undefined
   d. Undefined

7. _____ are the basic objects of study in graph theory. Informally speaking, a graph is a set of objects called points, nodes, or vertices connected by links called lines or edges.
   a. Thing
   b. Graphs7
   c. Undefined
   d. Undefined

8. A _____ is a symbolic representation denoting a quantity or expression. It often represents an "unknown" quantity that has the potential to change.
   a. Variable8
   b. Thing
   c. Undefined
   d. Undefined

9. A _____ is a set of numbers that designate location in a given reference system, such as x,y in a planar _____ system or an x,y,z in a three-dimensional _____ system.
   a. Coordinate9
   b. Thing
   c. Undefined
   d. Undefined

10. _____ is either of the two parts into which a plane divides the three-dimensional space. More generally, a _____ is either of the two parts into which a hyperplane divides an affine space.
   a. Half-space10
   b. Thing
   c. Undefined
   d. Undefined

11. In mathematics, a _____ is a partially ordered set (or poset) in which every pair of elements has a unique supremum (the elements' least upper bound; called their join) and an infimum (greatest lower bound; called their meet).

a. Lattice11
b. Concept
c. Undefined
d. Undefined

12. In mathematics, the _____ of a coordinate system is the point where the axes of the system intersect.
a. Thing
b. Origin12
c. Undefined
d. Undefined

13. A _____ consists of one quarter of the coordinate plane.
a. Thing
b. Quadrant13
c. Undefined
d. Undefined

14. Any point where a graph makes contact with an coordinate axis is called an _____ of the graph
a. Thing
b. Intercept14
c. Undefined
d. Undefined

15. A _____ can be described as an infinitely thin, infinitely long, perfectly straight curve containing an infinite number of points.
a. Line15
b. Thing
c. Undefined
d. Undefined

16. In mathematics, _____ are two-dimensional manifolds or surfaces that are perfectly flat.

Chapter 2. Functions and Graphs

a. Thing
b. Planes16
c. Undefined
d. Undefined

17. A spatial _____ is a concept used to define an exact location in space. It has no volume, area or length.
a. Thing
b. Point17
c. Undefined
d. Undefined

18. The _____ is the horizontal axis of a two-dimensional plot in the Cartesian coordinate system, that is typically pointed to the right. Also known as a right-handed coordinate system.
a. Thing
b. X-axis18
c. Undefined
d. Undefined

19. In reference to a 2D and 3D plane, the _____ is the vertical height of a 2D or 3D object.
a. Thing
b. Y-axis19
c. Undefined
d. Undefined

20. In astronomy, geography, geometry and related sciences and contexts, a plane is said to be _____ at a given point if it is locally perpendicular to the gradient of the gravity field, i.e., with the direction of the gravitational force at that point.
a. Thing
b. Horizontal20
c. Undefined
d. Undefined

21. In topology, the _____ are subsets S of a topological space X is the set of points which can be approached both from S and from the outside of S.

Chapter 2. Functions and Graphs

   a. Boundaries21
   b. Thing
   c. Undefined
   d. Undefined

22. If the function is mapping from real numbers to real numbers, its zeros are the points where its graph meets the x-axis. In this situation, a root can be called an _____.
   a. X-intercept22
   b. Thing
   c. Undefined
   d. Undefined

23. In two-dimensional coordinate geometry, the _____ is the point where the graph of a function or relation intercepts the y-axis of the coordinate system.
   a. Thing
   b. Y-intercept23
   c. Undefined
   d. Undefined

24. _____ is often used to describe the measurement of the steepness, incline, gradient, or grade of a straight line. The _____ is defined as the ratio of the "rise" divided by the "run" between two points on a line, or in other words, the ratio of the altitude change to the horizontal distance between any two points on the line.
   a. Thing
   b. Slope24
   c. Undefined
   d. Undefined

25. A _____ is a special kind of ratio, indicating a relationship between two measurements with different units, such as miles to gallons or cents to pounds.
   a. Rate25
   b. Thing
   c. Undefined
   d. Undefined

26. A _____ is one of the basic shapes of geometry: a polygon with three vertices and three sides which are straight line segments.

a. Triangle26
b. Thing
c. Undefined
d. Undefined

27. In mathematics and in the sciences, a _____ is a concise way of expressing information symbolically or a general relationship between quantities.
a. Formula27
b. Thing
c. Undefined
d. Undefined

28. The existence and properties of _____ are the basis of Euclid's parallel postulate. _____ are two lines on the same plane that do not intersect even assuming that lines extend to infinity in either direction.
a. Parallel lines28
b. Thing
c. Undefined
d. Undefined

29. In geometry, two lines or planes if one falls on the other in such a way as to create congruent adjacent angles. The term may be used as a noun or adjective. Thus, referring to Figure 1, the line AB is the _____ to CD through the point B.
a. Thing
b. Perpendicular29
c. Undefined
d. Undefined

30. In mathematics, an _____, mean, or central tendency of a data set refers to a measure of the "middle" or "expected" value of the data set.
a. Average30
b. Concept
c. Undefined
d. Undefined

31. A _____ is a part of a line that is bounded by two end points, and contains every point on the line between its end points.

Chapter 2. Functions and Graphs

   a. Thing
   b. Line segment31
   c. Undefined
   d. Undefined

32. _____ is the middle point of a line segment.
   a. Thing
   b. Midpoint32
   c. Undefined
   d. Undefined

33. In neutral geometry, the minimum _____ between two points is the length of the line segment between them.
   a. Thing
   b. Distance33
   c. Undefined
   d. Undefined

34. In mathematics, the multiplicative inverse of a number x, denoted 1/x or x^{-1}, is the number which, when multiplied by x, yields 1. The multiplicative inverse of x is also called the _____ of x.
   a. Thing
   b. Reciprocal34
   c. Undefined
   d. Undefined

35. In geometry, a line _____ is a part of a line that is bounded by two end points, and contains every point on the line between its end points.
   a. Concept
   b. Segment35
   c. Undefined
   d. Undefined

36. _____ is the fee paid on borrowed money.

Chapter 2. Functions and Graphs

   a. Interest36
   b. Thing
   c. Undefined
   d. Undefined

37. _____ is a statistical measure of the average length of survival of a living thing.
   a. Life expectancy37
   b. Thing
   c. Undefined
   d. Undefined

38. Leonhard _____ was a pioneering Swiss mathematician and physicist, who spent most of his life in Russia and Germany.
   a. Euler38
   b. Person
   c. Undefined
   d. Undefined

39. _____ was a pioneering Swiss mathematician and physicist, who spent most of his life in Russia and Germany
   a. Euler Leonhard39
   b. Person
   c. Undefined
   d. Undefined

40. In mathematics, the _____ of a function is the set of all "output" values produced by that function. Given a function $f : A \to B$, the _____ of f, is defined to be the set $\{x \in B : x = f(a) \text{ for some } a \in A\}$.
   a. Thing
   b. Range40
   c. Undefined
   d. Undefined

41. In mathematics, the concept of a _____ is a generalization of 2-place relations, such as the _____ of equality, denoted by the sign "=" in a statement like "5 + 7 = 12," or the _____ of order, denoted by the sign "<" in a statement like "5 < 12".

a. Relation41
b. Thing
c. Undefined
d. Undefined

42. Mathematical _____ is used in mathematics, and throughout the physical sciences, engineering, and economics. The complexity of such _____ ranges from relatively simple symbolic representations, such as numbers 1 and 2; function symbols sin and +, to conceptual symbols, such as lim and dy/dx; to equations and variables.
   a. Thing
   b. Notation42
   c. Undefined
   d. Undefined

43. In mathematics, the _____ is a conic section generated by the intersection of a right circular conical surface and a plane parallel to a generating straight line of that surface. It can also be defined as locus of points in a plane which are equidistant from a given point.
   a. Parabola43
   b. Thing
   c. Undefined
   d. Undefined

44. The mathematical concept of a _____ expresses the intuitive idea of deterministic dependence between two quantities, one of which is viewed as primary and the other as secondary. A _____ then is a way to associate a unique output for each input of a specified type, for example, a real number or an element of a given set.
   a. Thing
   b. Function44
   c. Undefined
   d. Undefined

45. _____ is a test to determine if a relation or its graph is a function or not
   a. Vertical line test45
   b. Thing
   c. Undefined
   d. Undefined

Chapter 2. Functions and Graphs

46. Acid _____ ratio measures the ability of a company to use its near cash or quick assets to immediately extinguish its current liabilities.
   a. Thing
   b. Test46
   c. Undefined
   d. Undefined

47. In mathematics, the _____ (or modulus) of a real number is its numerical value without regard to its sign.
   a. Absolute value47
   b. Thing
   c. Undefined
   d. Undefined

48. In geometry, a _____ is a special kind of point, usually a corner of a polygon, polyhedron, or higher dimensional polytope. In the geometry of curves a _____ is a point of where the first derivative of curvature is zero. In graph theory, a _____ is the fundamental unit out of which graphs are formed
   a. Thing
   b. Vertex48
   c. Undefined
   d. Undefined

49. _____ commonly refers to the 'output' of a function.
   a. Thing
   b. Value49
   c. Undefined
   d. Undefined

50. In financial mathematics, the _____ volatility of an option contract is the volatility _____ by the market price of the option based on an option pricing model.
   a. Thing
   b. Implied50
   c. Undefined
   d. Undefined

Chapter 2. Functions and Graphs

51. In mathematics, a _____ of a k-place relation $L \subseteq X_1 \times \ldots \times X_k$ is one of the sets X_j, $1 \le j \le k$. In the special case where k = 2 and $L \subseteq X_1 \times X_2$ is a function $L : X_1 \to X_2$, it is conventional to refer to X_1 as the _____ of the function and to refer to X_2 as the codomain of the function.
   a. Domain51
   b. Thing
   c. Undefined
   d. Undefined

52. In geographic information systems, a _____ comprises an entity with a geographic location, typically determined by points, arcs, or polygons. Carriageways and cadastres exemplify _____ data.
   a. Feature52
   b. Thing
   c. Undefined
   d. Undefined

53. _____ is, or relates to, the _____ temperature scale .
   a. Celsius53
   b. Thing
   c. Undefined
   d. Undefined

54. _____ is a concept in traditional logic referring to a "type of immediate inference in which from a given proposition another proposition is inferred which has as its subject the predicate of the original proposition and as its predicate the subject of the original proposition (the quality of the proposition being retained)."
   a. Concept
   b. Conversion54
   c. Undefined
   d. Undefined

55. _____ is a temperature scale named after the German physicist Daniel Gabriel _____ , who proposed it in 1724.
   a. Fahrenheit55
   b. Thing
   c. Undefined
   d. Undefined

Chapter 2. Functions and Graphs

56. The _____ expresses the fact that the difference in the y coordinate between two points on a line that is, y − y1 is proportional to the difference in the x coordinate that is, x − x1. The proportionality constant is m (the slope of the line.
   a. Thing
   b. Point-slope form56
   c. Undefined
   d. Undefined

57. _____ is a term used in accounting, economics and finance with reference to the fact that assets with finite lives lose value over time.
   a. Depreciation57
   b. Thing
   c. Undefined
   d. Undefined

58. In mathematics, _____ is the process of constructing new data points outside a discrete set of known data points. It is similar to the process of interpolation, which constructs new points between known points, but its results are often less meaningful, and are subject to greater uncertainty.
   a. Thing
   b. Extrapolation58
   c. Undefined
   d. Undefined

59. _____ is a method of constructing new data points from a discrete set of known data points.
   a. Thing
   b. Interpolation59
   c. Undefined
   d. Undefined

60. _____ is a trigonometric function that is the reciprocal of cosine.
   a. Secant60
   b. Thing
   c. Undefined
   d. Undefined

61. _____ of a curve is a line that intersects two or more points on the curve.

Chapter 2. Functions and Graphs

   a. Secant line61
   b. Thing
   c. Undefined
   d. Undefined

62. The _____ of a ring R is defined to be the smallest positive integer n such that $n\,a = 0$, for all a in R.
   a. Characteristic62
   b. Thing
   c. Undefined
   d. Undefined

63. _____ is a notation for writing numbers that is often used by scientists and mathematicians to make it easier to write large and small numbers.
   a. Thing
   b. Scientific notation63
   c. Undefined
   d. Undefined

64. A _____ is a polynomial function of the form $f(x) = ax^2 + bx + c$, where a, b, c are real numbers and a , 0.
   a. Event
   b. Quadratic function64
   c. Undefined
   d. Undefined

65. An _____ is a straight line around which a geometric figure can be rotated.
   a. Thing
   b. Axis65
   c. Undefined
   d. Undefined

66. _____ of a two-dimensional figure is a line such that, if a perpendicular is constructed, any two points lying on the perpendicular at equal distances from the _____ are identical.

Chapter 2. Functions and Graphs

   a. Axis of symmetry66
   b. Thing
   c. Undefined
   d. Undefined

67. The word _____ means curving in or hollowed inward.
   a. Concavity67
   b. Thing
   c. Undefined
   d. Undefined

68. In mathematics and more specifically set theory, the _____ set is the unique set which contains no elements.
   a. Thing
   b. Empty68
   c. Undefined
   d. Undefined

69. In mathematics and more specifically set theory, the _____ is the unique set which contains no elements.
   a. Thing
   b. Empty set69
   c. Undefined
   d. Undefined

70. In measure theory, a _____ is a set that is negligible for the purposes of the measure in question.
   a. Null set70
   b. Concept
   c. Undefined
   d. Undefined

71. _____ means "constancy", i.e. if something retains a certain feature even after we change a way of looking at it, then it is symmetric.

a. Thing
b. Symmetry71
c. Undefined
d. Undefined

72. In mathematics, a _____ can be thought of as any collection of distinct objects considered as a whole.
a. Thing
b. Set72
c. Undefined
d. Undefined

73. In plane geometry, a _____ is a polygon with four equal sides, four right angles, and parallel opposite sides. In algebra, the _____ of a number is that number multiplied by itself.
a. Thing
b. Square73
c. Undefined
d. Undefined

74. In mathematics, a _____ of a number x is a number r such that $r^2 = x$, or in words, a number r whose square (the result of multiplying the number by itself) is x.
a. Thing
b. Square root74
c. Undefined
d. Undefined

75. In mathematics, a _____ of a complex-valued function f is a member x of the domain of f such that f(x) vanishes at x, that is, $x : f(x) = 0$.
a. Root75
b. Thing
c. Undefined
d. Undefined

76. A _____ of a number is a number a such that $a^3 = x$.

Chapter 2. Functions and Graphs

a. Thing
b. Cube root76
c. Undefined
d. Undefined

77. A _____ function is a function for which, intuitively, small changes in the input result in small changes in the output.
a. Continuous77
b. Event
c. Undefined
d. Undefined

78. _____ of an object is its speed in a particular direction.
a. Thing
b. Velocity78
c. Undefined
d. Undefined

79. A _____ typically refers to a class of handheld calculators that are capable of plotting graphs, solving equation systems, and performing numerous other tasks with variables.
a. Thing
b. Graphing calculator79
c. Undefined
d. Undefined

80. _____ has many meanings, most of which simply .
a. Thing
b. Power80
c. Undefined
d. Undefined

81. _____ is both a number and a numerical digit used to represent that number in numerals. As a number, it means nothing — an absence of other values.

a. Thing
b. Zero81
c. Undefined
d. Undefined

82. In elementary algebra, an _____ is a set that contains every real number between two indicated numbers and may contain the two numbers themselves.
a. Thing
b. Interval82
c. Undefined
d. Undefined

83. In mathematics, a _____ is a number, function, or distribution which satisfies an equation.
a. Solution83
b. Thing
c. Undefined
d. Undefined

84. In linear algebra, the _____ of an n-by-n square matrix A is defined to be the sum of the elements on the main diagonal of A,
a. Thing
b. TRACE84
c. Undefined
d. Undefined

85. _____ is an adjective usually refering to being in the centre.
a. Thing
b. Central85
c. Undefined
d. Undefined

86. _____ systems represent systems whose behavior is not expressible as a sum of the behaviors of its descriptors.

Chapter 2. Functions and Graphs

a. Thing
b. Nonlinear86
c. Undefined
d. Undefined

87. In probability theory and statistics, _____, also called _____ coefficient, indicates the strength and direction of a linear relationship between two random variables.
a. Thing
b. Correlation87
c. Undefined
d. Undefined

88. In mathematics, a _____ is a constant multiplicative factor of a certain object. The object can be such things as a variable, a vector, a function, etc. For example, the _____ of $9x^2$ is 9.
a. Thing
b. Coefficient88
c. Undefined
d. Undefined

89. _____ is a synonym for information.
a. Thing
b. Data89
c. Undefined
d. Undefined

90. _____ is a regression method that models the relationship between a dependent variable Y, independent variables Xp, and a random term å.
a. Linear regression90
b. Thing
c. Undefined
d. Undefined

91. In Euclidean geometry, a uniform _____ is a linear transformation that enlargers or diminishes objects, and whose _____ factor is the same in all directions. This is also called homothethy.

Chapter 2. Functions and Graphs

   a. Scale91
   b. Thing
   c. Undefined
   d. Undefined

92. _____ is the portion of a solid – normally a cone or pyramid – which lies between two parallel planes cutting the solid.
   a. Thing
   b. Truncated pyramid92
   c. Undefined
   d. Undefined

93. _____ is the measurement of distance between a specified point and a corresponding plane of reference. If the distance is occupied by a contiguous form of matter, the measurement is colloquially known as how "tall" the form is.
   a. Thing
   b. Height93
   c. Undefined
   d. Undefined

94. The _____ of a solid object is the three-dimensional concept of how much space it occupies, often quantified numerically.
   a. Volume94
   b. Thing
   c. Undefined
   d. Undefined

95. A _____ is a first degree polynomial mathematical function of the form: f(x) = mx + b where m and b are real constants and x is a real variable.
   a. Linear function95
   b. Thing
   c. Undefined
   d. Undefined

96. _____ is the act of transforming data with the aim of extracting useful information and facilitating conclusions.

a. Concept
b. Data analysis96
c. Undefined
d. Undefined

Chapter 3. Operations on Functions and Analyzing Graphs

1. In abstract algebra, _____ consists of sets with binary operations that satisfy certain axioms.
   a. Grouping1
   b. Thing
   c. Undefined
   d. Undefined

2. _____ numerals are a numeral system originating in ancient Rome, adapted from Etruscan numerals.
   a. Roman2
   b. Thing
   c. Undefined
   d. Undefined

3. _____ are objects, characters, or other concrete representations of ideas, concepts, or other abstractions.
   a. Symbols3
   b. Thing
   c. Undefined
   d. Undefined

4. _____ is one of the four basic arithmetic operations; it is essentially the opposite of addition.
   a. Subtraction4
   b. Thing
   c. Undefined
   d. Undefined

5. The mathematical concept of a _____ expresses the intuitive idea of deterministic dependence between two quantities, one of which is viewed as primary and the other as secondary. A _____ then is a way to associate a unique output for each input of a specified type, for example, a real number or an element of a given set.
   a. Function5
   b. Thing
   c. Undefined
   d. Undefined

6. A _____ is a symbol or group of symbols, or a word in a natural language that represents a number.

Chapter 3. Operations on Functions and Analyzing Graphs

a. Thing
b. Numeral6
c. Undefined
d. Undefined

7. A _____ is the result of the addition of a set of numbers. The numbers may be natural numbers, complex numbers, matrices, or still more complicated objects. An infinite _____ is a subtle procedure known as a series.
a. Thing
b. Sum7
c. Undefined
d. Undefined

8. In mathematics, a _____ is the result of multiplying, or an expression that identifies factors to be multiplied.
a. Product8
b. Thing
c. Undefined
d. Undefined

9. In mathematics, a _____ is the end result of a division problem. It can also be expressed as the number of times the divisor divides into the dividend.
a. Thing
b. Quotient9
c. Undefined
d. Undefined

10. In mathematics, especially in elementary arithmetic, _____ is an arithmetic operation which is the inverse of multiplication.
a. Thing
b. Division10
c. Undefined
d. Undefined

11. In mathematics, a _____ is an expression that is constructed from one or more variables and constants, using only the operations of addition, subtraction, multiplication, and constant positive whole number exponents. is a _____. Note in particular that division by an expression containing a variable is not in general allowed in polynomials.

Chapter 3. Operations on Functions and Analyzing Graphs

a. Polynomial11
b. Thing
c. Undefined
d. Undefined

12. In mathematics, a _____ of a positive integer n is a way of writing n as a sum of positive integers.
a. Composition12
b. Thing
c. Undefined
d. Undefined

13. A _____ number is a positive integer which has a positive divisor other than one or itself.
a. Composite13
b. Thing
c. Undefined
d. Undefined

14. A _____, formed by the composition of one function on another, represents the application of the former to the result of the application of the latter to the argument of the composite.
a. Composite function14
b. Thing
c. Undefined
d. Undefined

15. A _____ typically refers to a class of handheld calculators that are capable of plotting graphs, solving equation systems, and performing numerous other tasks with variables.
a. Graphing calculator15
b. Thing
c. Undefined
d. Undefined

16. _____ refers to the reduction of the body of a formerly living organism into simpler forms of matter.

Chapter 3. Operations on Functions and Analyzing Graphs 61

   a. Thing
   b. Decomposing16
   c. Undefined
   d. Undefined

17. In mathematics, a _____ of a k-place relation $L \subseteq X_1 \times ... \times X_k$ is one of the sets X_j, $1 \leq j \leq k$. In the special case where k = 2 and $L \subseteq X_1 \times X_2$ is a function $L : X_1 \to X_2$, it is conventional to refer to X_1 as the _____ of the function and to refer to X_2 as the codomain of the function.
   a. Thing
   b. Domain17
   c. Undefined
   d. Undefined

18. _____ interest refers to the fact that whenever interest is calculated, it is based not only on the original principal, but also on any unpaid interest that has been added to the principal.
   a. Compound18
   b. Thing
   c. Undefined
   d. Undefined

19. In mathematics, a _____ is a quadric surface, with the following equation in Cartesian coordinates: $(x/_a)^2 + (y/_b)^2 = 1$.
   a. Cylinder19
   b. Thing
   c. Undefined
   d. Undefined

20. _____ is a physical quantity expressing the size of a part of a surface. The term can also be used in a non-mathematical context to be mean "vicinity".
   a. Area20
   b. Thing
   c. Undefined
   d. Undefined

21. In mathematics, specifically in topology, a _____ is a two-dimensional manifold. The most familiar examples are those that arise as the boundaries of solid objects in ordinary three-dimensional Euclidean space, E^3.

Chapter 3. Operations on Functions and Analyzing Graphs

  a. Thing
  b. Surface21
  c. Undefined
  d. Undefined

22. _____ element of an element x with respect to a binary operation * with identity element e is an element y such that x * y = y * x = e. In particular,
  a. Thing
  b. Inverse22
  c. Undefined
  d. Undefined

23. An _____ is a function which does the reverse of a given function.
  a. Inverse function23
  b. Thing
  c. Undefined
  d. Undefined

24. _____ correspondence is the pairing off of one set to another such that each member of the first has exactly one counterpart in the second and each member of the second has exactly one counterpart in the first.
  a. One-to-one24
  b. Thing
  c. Undefined
  d. Undefined

25. In astronomy, geography, geometry and related sciences and contexts, a plane is said to be _____ at a given point if it is locally perpendicular to the gradient of the gravity field, i.e., with the direction of the gravitational force at that point.
  a. Horizontal25
  b. Thing
  c. Undefined
  d. Undefined

26. _____ is a test used to determine if a function is injective, surjective or bijective.

Chapter 3. Operations on Functions and Analyzing Graphs 63

   a. Thing
   b. Horizontal line test26
   c. Undefined
   d. Undefined

27. Acid _____ ratio measures the ability of a company to use its near cash or quick assets to immediately extinguish its current liabilities.
   a. Test27
   b. Thing
   c. Undefined
   d. Undefined

28. _____ are the basic objects of study in graph theory. Informally speaking, a graph is a set of objects called points, nodes, or vertices connected by links called lines or edges.
   a. Thing
   b. Graphs28
   c. Undefined
   d. Undefined

29. In mathematics, a _____ is the set of all points in three-dimensional space (R^3) which are at distance r from a fixed point of that space, where r is a positive real number called the radius of the _____. The fixed point is called the center or centre, and is not part of the _____ itself.
   a. Thing
   b. Sphere29
   c. Undefined
   d. Undefined

30. _____ is the measurement of distance between a specified point and a corresponding plane of reference. If the distance is occupied by a contiguous form of matter, the measurement is colloquially known as how "tall" the form is.
   a. Height30
   b. Thing
   c. Undefined
   d. Undefined

31. In mathematics, _____ is a part of the set theoretic notion of function.

a. Thing
b. Image31
c. Undefined
d. Undefined

32. In classical geometry, a _____ of a circle or sphere is any line segment from its center to its boundary. By extension, the _____ of a circle or sphere is the length of any such segment. The _____ is half the diameter. In science and engineering the term _____ of curvature is commonly used as a synonym for _____.
   a. Radius32
   b. Thing
   c. Undefined
   d. Undefined

33. A _____ is a special kind of ratio, indicating a relationship between two measurements with different units, such as miles to gallons or cents to pounds.
   a. Rate33
   b. Thing
   c. Undefined
   d. Undefined

34. In Euclidean geometry, a _____ is moving every point a constant distance in a specified direction.
   a. Concept
   b. Translation34
   c. Undefined
   d. Undefined

35. In mathematics, a _____ in elementary terms is any of a variety of different functions from geometry, such as rotations, reflections and translations.
   a. Thing
   b. Transformation35
   c. Undefined
   d. Undefined

36. In mathematics, a _____ (also spelled reflexion) is a map that transforms an object into its mirror image.

a. Concept
b. Reflection36
c. Undefined
d. Undefined

37. The _____ is the horizontal axis of a two- dimensional plot in the Cartesian coordinate system, that is typically pointed to the right. Also known as a right-handed coordinate system.
a. Thing
b. X-axis37
c. Undefined
d. Undefined

38. In mathematics, suppose C is a collection of mathematical objects . Then we say that C is _____ if every c ∊ C is uniquely determined by less information about c than one would expect.
a. Rigid38
b. Thing
c. Undefined
d. Undefined

39. In mathematics, _____ are the intuitive idea of a geometrical one-dimensional and continuous object.
a. Thing
b. Curves39
c. Undefined
d. Undefined

40. In mathematics and in the sciences, a _____ is a concise way of expressing information symbolically or a general relationship between quantities.
a. Thing
b. Formula40
c. Undefined
d. Undefined

41. The _____ of a solid object is the three-dimensional concept of how much space it occupies, often quantified numerically.

Chapter 3. Operations on Functions and Analyzing Graphs

   a. Thing
   b. Volume41
   c. Undefined
   d. Undefined

42. _____ is a technique used in algebra to solve quadratic equations, in analytic geometry for determining the shapes of graphs, and in calculus for computing integrals, including, but hardly limited to, the integrals that define Laplace transforms. The essential objective is to reduce a quadratic polynomial in a variable in an equation or expression to a squared polynomial of linear order. This can reduce an equation or integral to one that is more easily solved or evaluated.
   a. Thing
   b. Completing the square42
   c. Undefined
   d. Undefined

43. An _____ is a mathematical statement, in symbols, that two things are the same or equivalent. Equations are written with an equal sign, as in 2 + 3 = 5.
   a. Thing
   b. Equation43
   c. Undefined
   d. Undefined

44. In mathematics, a _____ is a polynomial equation of the second degree. The general form is $ax^2 + bx + c = 0$.
   a. Thing
   b. Quadratic equation44
   c. Undefined
   d. Undefined

45. A _____ is a polynomial function of the form $f(x) = ax^2 + bx + c$, where a, b, c are real numbers and a , 0.
   a. Quadratic function45
   b. Event
   c. Undefined
   d. Undefined

46. In plane geometry, a _____ is a polygon with four equal sides, four right angles, and parallel opposite sides. In algebra, the _____ of a number is that number multiplied by itself.

Chapter 3. Operations on Functions and Analyzing Graphs

a. Thing
b. Square46
c. Undefined
d. Undefined

47. In geometry, a _____ is a special kind of point, usually a corner of a polygon, polyhedron, or higher dimensional polytope. In the geometry of curves a _____ is a point of where the first derivative of curvature is zero. In graph theory, a _____ is the fundamental unit out of which graphs are formed
  a. Vertex47
  b. Thing
  c. Undefined
  d. Undefined

48. The term _____ refers to the largest and the smallest element of a set.
  a. Extreme value48
  b. Thing
  c. Undefined
  d. Undefined

49. _____ commonly refers to the 'output' of a function.
  a. Value49
  b. Thing
  c. Undefined
  d. Undefined

50. In mathematics, an _____ number is any real number that is not a rational number- that is, it is a number which cannot be expressed as a fraction m/n, where m and n are integers.
  a. Irrational50
  b. Thing
  c. Undefined
  d. Undefined

51. The act of _____ is the calculated approximation of a result which is usable even if input data may be incomplete, uncertain, or noisy.

Chapter 3. Operations on Functions and Analyzing Graphs

a. Thing
b. Estimating51
c. Undefined
d. Undefined

52. In mathematics, a _____ of a complex-valued function f is a member x of the domain of f such that f(x) vanishes at x, that is, x : f (x) = 0.
    a. Root52
    b. Thing
    c. Undefined
    d. Undefined

53. The _____ are the only integral domain whose positive elements are well-ordered, and in which order is preserved by addition. Like the natural numbers, the _____ form a countably infinite set. The set of all _____ is usually denoted in mathematics by a boldface Z .
    a. Integers53
    b. Thing
    c. Undefined
    d. Undefined

54. In mathematics, a _____ number is a number which can be expressed as a ratio of two integers. Non-integer _____ numbers (commonly called fractions) are usually written as the vulgar fraction a / b, where b is not zero.
    a. Thing
    b. Rational54
    c. Undefined
    d. Undefined

55. In mathematics, a _____ is any function which can be written as the ratio of two polynomial functions.
    a. Rational function55
    b. Thing
    c. Undefined
    d. Undefined

56. In mathematics, the multiplicative inverse of a number x, denoted 1/x or x^{-1}, is the number which, when multiplied by x, yields 1. The multiplicative inverse of x is also called the _____ of x.

Chapter 3. Operations on Functions and Analyzing Graphs

a. Reciprocal56
b. Thing
c. Undefined
d. Undefined

57. Mathematical _____ is used in mathematics, and throughout the physical sciences, engineering, and economics. The complexity of such _____ ranges from relatively simple symbolic representations, such as numbers 1 and 2; function symbols sin and +, to conceptual symbols, such as lim and dy/dx; to equations and variables.
   a. Notation57
   b. Thing
   c. Undefined
   d. Undefined

58. An _____ is a straight line or curve A to which another curve B approaches closer and closer as one moves along it. As one moves along B, the space between it and the _____ A becomes smaller and smaller, and can in fact be made as small as one could wish by going far enough along. A curve may or may not touch or cross its _____. In fact, the curve may intersect the _____ an infinite number of times.
   a. Thing
   b. Asymptote58
   c. Undefined
   d. Undefined

59. _____ is a straight line or curve A to which another curve B the one being studied approaches closer and closer as one moves along it.
   a. Vertical asymptote59
   b. Thing
   c. Undefined
   d. Undefined

60. A circular _____ or circle _____ also known as a pie piece is the portion of a circle enclosed by two radii and an arc.
   a. Sector60
   b. Thing
   c. Undefined
   d. Undefined

Chapter 3. Operations on Functions and Analyzing Graphs

61. _____ consists of the first element in a coordinate pair. When graphed in the coordinate plane, it is the distance from the y-axis. Frequently called the x coordinate.
   a. Abscissa61
   b. Thing
   c. Undefined
   d. Undefined

62. The _____ is the y- coordinate of a point within a two dimensional coordinate system. It is sometimes used to refer to the axis rather than the distance along the coordinate system.
   a. Thing
   b. Ordinate62
   c. Undefined
   d. Undefined

63. In mathematics and the mathematical sciences, a _____ is a fixed, but possibly unspecified, value. This is in contrast to a variable, which is not fixed.
   a. Thing
   b. Constant63
   c. Undefined
   d. Undefined

64. In mathematics and logic, a _____ proof is a way of showing the truth or falsehood of a given statement by a straightforward combination of established facts, usually existing lemmas and theorems, without making any further assumptions.
   a. Thing
   b. Direct64
   c. Undefined
   d. Undefined

65. _____ is the relationship between two variables, like a ratio in which the two quantities being compared are different units.
   a. Direct variation65
   b. Thing
   c. Undefined
   d. Undefined

Chapter 3. Operations on Functions and Analyzing Graphs

66. _____ is a special mathematical relationship between two quantities. Two quantities are called proportional if they vary in such a way that one of the quantities is a constant multiple of the other, or equivalently if they have a constant ratio.
a. Proportionality66
b. Thing
c. Undefined
d. Undefined

67. _____ is one of the gas laws. It states that: " For a fixed mass of ideal gas at fixed temperature, the product of pressure and volume is a constant. "
a. Thing
b. Boyle's law67
c. Undefined
d. Undefined

68. _____ is a relationship among three or more variables in which each pair of variables varies directly or inversely.
a. Thing
b. Joint variation68
c. Undefined
d. Undefined

69. _____ is a synonym for information.
a. Thing
b. Data69
c. Undefined
d. Undefined

70. _____ is the act of transforming data with the aim of extracting useful information and facilitating conclusions.
a. Concept
b. Data analysis70
c. Undefined
d. Undefined

71. _____ has many meanings, most of which simply .

Chapter 3. Operations on Functions and Analyzing Graphs

a. Thing
b. Power71
c. Undefined
d. Undefined

72. In physics, _____ is an influence that may cause an object to accelerate. It may be experienced as a lift, a push, or a pull. The actual acceleration of the body is determined by the vector sum of all forces acting on it, known as net _____ or resultant _____.
a. Thing
b. Force72
c. Undefined
d. Undefined

73. _____ is the fee paid on borrowed money.
a. Interest73
b. Thing
c. Undefined
d. Undefined

74. An _____ is the fee paid on borrow money.
a. Concept
b. Interest rate74
c. Undefined
d. Undefined

75. A _____ function is a function for which, intuitively, small changes in the input result in small changes in the output.
a. Continuous75
b. Event
c. Undefined
d. Undefined

76. A _____ is a function for which, intuitively, small changes in the input result in small changes in the output.

Chapter 3. Operations on Functions and Analyzing Graphs

a. Event
b. Continuous function76
c. Undefined
d. Undefined

77. _____ is a method of describing limiting behavior.
a. Thing
b. Asymptotic77
c. Undefined
d. Undefined

78. A _____ represents a system whose behavior is not expressible as a sum of the behaviors of its descriptors.
a. Nonlinear system78
b. Thing
c. Undefined
d. Undefined

79. Continuous functions are of utmost importance in mathematics and applications. However, not all functions are continuous. If a function is not continuous at a point in its domain, one says that it has a _____ there. The set of all points of _____ of a function may be a discrete set, a dense set, or even the entire domain of the function.
a. Thing
b. Discontinuity79
c. Undefined
d. Undefined

80. _____ systems represent systems whose behavior is not expressible as a sum of the behaviors of its descriptors.
a. Thing
b. Nonlinear80
c. Undefined
d. Undefined

81. _____ are a set of equations containing multiple variables.

Chapter 3. Operations on Functions and Analyzing Graphs

  a. Systems of equations81
  b. Thing
  c. Undefined
  d. Undefined

82. A function on the real numbers is called a _____ if it can be written as a finite linear combination of indicator functions of half-open intervals.
  a. Thing
  b. Step function82
  c. Undefined
  d. Undefined

83. In mathematics, the _____ (or modulus) of a real number is its numerical value without regard to its sign.
  a. Thing
  b. Absolute value83
  c. Undefined
  d. Undefined

84. In mathematics, _____ and odd functions are functions which satisfy particular symmetry relations, with respect to taking additive inverses.
  a. Even functions84
  b. Thing
  c. Undefined
  d. Undefined

85. _____ means "constancy", i.e. if something retains a certain feature even after we change a way of looking at it, then it is symmetric.
  a. Thing
  b. Symmetry85
  c. Undefined
  d. Undefined

86. In mathematics, the _____ of a coordinate system is the point where the axes of the system intersect.

Chapter 3. Operations on Functions and Analyzing Graphs

a. Origin86
b. Thing
c. Undefined
d. Undefined

87. In elementary algebra, an _____ is a set that contains every real number between two indicated numbers and may contain the two numbers themselves.
a. Interval87
b. Thing
c. Undefined
d. Undefined

88. The _____ of a member of a multiset is how many memberships in the multiset it has.
a. Thing
b. Multiplicity88
c. Undefined
d. Undefined

89. In mathematics, a _____ is a statement that can be proved on the basis of explicitly stated or previously agreed assumptions.
a. Theorem89
b. Thing
c. Undefined
d. Undefined

90. _____ is both a number and a numerical digit used to represent that number in numerals. As a number, it means nothing — an absence of other values.
a. Thing
b. Zero90
c. Undefined
d. Undefined

91. The function difference divided by the point difference is known as the _____

a. Difference quotient91
b. Thing
c. Undefined
d. Undefined

92. In mathematics, the _____ functions are functions of an angle; they are important when studying triangles and modeling periodic phenomena, among many other applications.
a. Trigonometric92
b. Thing
c. Undefined
d. Undefined

93. In mathematics, a _____ section is a curve that can be formed by intersecting a cone with a plane.
a. Conic93
b. Thing
c. Undefined
d. Undefined

94. In mathematics, a _____ is a curve that can be formed by intersecting a cone with a plane.
a. Thing
b. Conic section94
c. Undefined
d. Undefined

95. A _____ is a deliberate process for transforming one or more inputs into one or more results.
a. Calculation95
b. Thing
c. Undefined
d. Undefined

96. In mathematics, a _____ set is the complement of a meager set. A meager set is one which is the countable union of nowhere dense sets.

a. Thing
b. Residual96
c. Undefined
d. Undefined

97. In arithmetic, the _____ refers to the number b in an expression of the form b^n.
a. Thing
b. Base97
c. Undefined
d. Undefined

98. In business, particularly accounting, a _____ is the time intervals that the accounts, statement, payments, or other calculations cover.
a. Thing
b. Period98
c. Undefined
d. Undefined

Chapter 4. Polynomial and Rational Functions

1. _____ is a payment made by a company to its shareholders
   a. Dividend1
   b. Thing
   c. Undefined
   d. Undefined

2. In mathematics, a _____ of an integer n, also called a factor of n, is an integer which evenly divides n without leaving a remainder.
   a. Divisor2
   b. Thing
   c. Undefined
   d. Undefined

3. A _____ is the part of the dividend that is left over when the dividend is not evenly divisible by the divisor.
   a. Remainder3
   b. Thing
   c. Undefined
   d. Undefined

4. In mathematics, especially in elementary arithmetic, _____ is an arithmetic operation which is the inverse of multiplication.
   a. Division4
   b. Thing
   c. Undefined
   d. Undefined

5. In mathematics, a _____ is an expression that is constructed from one or more variables and constants, using only the operations of addition, subtraction, multiplication, and constant positive whole number exponents. is a _____. Note in particular that division by an expression containing a variable is not in general allowed in polynomials.
   a. Polynomial5
   b. Thing
   c. Undefined
   d. Undefined

6. In mathematics, a _____ is the end result of a division problem. It can also be expressed as the number of times the divisor divides into the dividend.

Chapter 4. Polynomial and Rational Functions

   a. Thing
   b. Quotient6
   c. Undefined
   d. Undefined

7. In mathematics, _____ allows the rapid division of any polynomial by a binomial of the form x − r. It was described by Paolo Ruffini in 1809. _____ is a special case of long division when the divisor is a linear factor.
   a. Thing
   b. Ruffini's rule7
   c. Undefined
   d. Undefined

8. In mathematics, factorization (British English: factorisation) or factoring is the decomposition of an object (for example, a number, a polynomial, or a matrix) into a product of other objects, or _____, which when multiplied together give the original.
   a. Thing
   b. Factors8
   c. Undefined
   d. Undefined

9. Acid _____ ratio measures the ability of a company to use its near cash or quick assets to immediately extinguish its current liabilities.
   a. Test9
   b. Thing
   c. Undefined
   d. Undefined

10. A _____ is a quadrilateral, which is defined as a shape with four sides, which has a pair of parallel sides.
   a. Thing
   b. Trapezoid10
   c. Undefined
   d. Undefined

11. _____ is a physical quantity expressing the size of a part of a surface. The term can also be used in a non-mathematical context to be mean "vicinity".

a. Area11
b. Thing
c. Undefined
d. Undefined

12. The _____ of a solid object is the three-dimensional concept of how much space it occupies, often quantified numerically.
a. Thing
b. Volume12
c. Undefined
d. Undefined

13. _____ in algebra is an application of polynomial long division.
a. Thing
b. Remainder theorem13
c. Undefined
d. Undefined

14. In mathematics, a _____ is a statement that can be proved on the basis of explicitly stated or previously agreed assumptions.
a. Thing
b. Theorem14
c. Undefined
d. Undefined

15. The _____ is a theorem for finding out the factors of a polynomial.
a. Thing
b. Factor theorem15
c. Undefined
d. Undefined

16. In mathematics, a _____ is a constant multiplicative factor of a certain object. The object can be such things as a variable, a vector, a function, etc. For example, the _____ of $9x^2$ is 9.

Chapter 4. Polynomial and Rational Functions

   a. Thing
   b. Coefficient16
   c. Undefined
   d. Undefined

17. In mathematics, a _____ is a number in the form of a + bi where a and b are real numbers, and i is the imaginary unit, with the property i 2 = −1. The real number a is called the real part of the _____, and the real number b is the imaginary part.
   a. Complex number17
   b. Thing
   c. Undefined
   d. Undefined

18. A _____ is a mathematical concept used to describe and assess quantity. It is an abstract entity representing a quantity, used to express how many are being referred to, or how much there is of some thing or property.
   a. Number18
   b. Thing
   c. Undefined
   d. Undefined

19. In mathematics, a _____ of a complex-valued function f is a member x of the domain of f such that f(x) vanishes at x, that is, x : f (x) = 0.
   a. Root19
   b. Thing
   c. Undefined
   d. Undefined

20. In algebra, a _____ is a binomial formed by taking the opposite of the second term of a binomial.
   a. Thing
   b. Conjugate20
   c. Undefined
   d. Undefined

21. The _____ of a member of a multiset is how many memberships in the multiset it has.

a. Thing
b. Multiplicity21
c. Undefined
d. Undefined

22. _____ is both a number and a numerical digit used to represent that number in numerals. As a number, it means nothing — an absence of other values.
a. Thing
b. Zero22
c. Undefined
d. Undefined

23. _____ is a branch of mathematics concerning the study of structure, relation and quantity.
a. Algebra23
b. Concept
c. Undefined
d. Undefined

24. In number theory, the _____ of arithmetic (or unique factorization theorem) states that every natural number greater than 1 can be written as a unique product of prime numbers.
a. Concept
b. Fundamental theorem24
c. Undefined
d. Undefined

25. _____ states that every non-zero single-variable polynomial, with complex coefficients, has exactly as many complex roots as its degree, if repeated roots are counted up to their multiplicity.
a. Thing
b. Fundamental theorem of algebra25
c. Undefined
d. Undefined

26. The mathematical concept of a _____ expresses the intuitive idea of deterministic dependence between two quantities, one of which is viewed as primary and the other as secondary. A _____ then is a way to associate a unique output for each input of a specified type, for example, a real number or an element of a given set.

a. Thing
b. Function26
c. Undefined
d. Undefined

27. The word _____ comes from the Latin word linearis, which means created by lines.
a. Linear27
b. Thing
c. Undefined
d. Undefined

28. In mathematics, _____ is the decomposition of an object into a product of other objects, or factors, which when multiplied together give the original.
a. Thing
b. Factoring28
c. Undefined
d. Undefined

29. The _____ implies that on any great circle around the world, the temperature, pressure, elevation, carbon dioxide concentration, or anything else that varies continuously, there will always exist two antipodal points that share the same value for that variable.
a. Intermediate value theorem29
b. Thing
c. Undefined
d. Undefined

30. A _____ is a mathematical statement which follows easily from a previously proven statement, typically a mathematical theorem.
a. Thing
b. Corollary30
c. Undefined
d. Undefined

31. In mathematics, a _____ number is a number which can be expressed as a ratio of two integers. Non-integer _____ numbers (commonly called fractions) are usually written as the vulgar fraction a / b, where b is not zero.

Chapter 4. Polynomial and Rational Functions

    a. Rational31
    b. Thing
    c. Undefined
    d. Undefined

32. _____ was a highly influential French philosopher, mathematician, scientist, and writer. Dubbed the "Founder of Modern Philosophy", and the "Father of Modern Mathematics". His theories provided the basis for the calculus of Newton and Leibniz, by applying infinitesimal calculus to the tangent line problem, thus permitting the evolution of that branch of modern mathematics
    a. Person
    b. Descartes32
    c. Undefined
    d. Undefined

33. The term _____ is defined dually as an element of P which is lesser than or equal to every element of S.
    a. Thing
    b. Lower bound33
    c. Undefined
    d. Undefined

34. In philosophy, mathematics, and logic, a _____ is an attribute of an object; thus a red object is said to have the _____ of redness.
    a. Thing
    b. Property34
    c. Undefined
    d. Undefined

35. A _____ typically refers to a class of handheld calculators that are capable of plotting graphs, solving equation systems, and performing numerous other tasks with variables.
    a. Thing
    b. Graphing calculator35
    c. Undefined
    d. Undefined

36. In mathematics, the _____ (or modulus) of a real number is its numerical value without regard to its sign.

Chapter 4. Polynomial and Rational Functions

  a. Thing
  b. Absolute value36
  c. Undefined
  d. Undefined

37. In plane geometry, a _____ is a polygon with four equal sides, four right angles, and parallel opposite sides. In algebra, the _____ of a number is that number multiplied by itself.
  a. Thing
  b. Square37
  c. Undefined
  d. Undefined

38. In mathematics, a _____ of a number x is a number r such that $r^2 = x$, or in words, a number r whose square (the result of multiplying the number by itself) is x.
  a. Thing
  b. Square root38
  c. Undefined
  d. Undefined

39. _____ commonly refers to the 'output' of a function.
  a. Value39
  b. Thing
  c. Undefined
  d. Undefined

40. _____ are the basic objects of study in graph theory. Informally speaking, a graph is a set of objects called points, nodes, or vertices connected by links called lines or edges.
  a. Thing
  b. Graphs40
  c. Undefined
  d. Undefined

41. In mathematics, the _____ of a coordinate system is the point where the axes of the system intersect.

86 Chapter 4. Polynomial and Rational Functions

a. Origin41
b. Thing
c. Undefined
d. Undefined

42. A _____ is any value or expression separated from another _____ by a + or - sign in an overall expression.
a. Thing
b. Term42
c. Undefined
d. Undefined

43. In mathematics and elsewhere, the adjective _____ means fourth order, such as the function x4. A _____ number is a number which equals the fourth power of an integer.
a. Quartic43
b. Thing
c. Undefined
d. Undefined

44. _____ has many meanings, most of which simply .
a. Power44
b. Thing
c. Undefined
d. Undefined

45. The term _____ refers to the largest and the smallest element of a set.
a. Thing
b. Extreme value45
c. Undefined
d. Undefined

46. A spatial _____ is a concept used to define an exact location in space. It has no volume, area or length.

Chapter 4. Polynomial and Rational Functions

   a. Thing
   b. Point46
   c. Undefined
   d. Undefined

47. _____ is a criterion for the convergence of an infinite series
   a. Thing
   b. Root test47
   c. Undefined
   d. Undefined

48. In geometry, _____ is the division of something into two equal parts, usually by a line.
   a. Bisection48
   b. Thing
   c. Undefined
   d. Undefined

49. _____ usually occurs when an exact form or an exact numerical number is unknown.
   a. Approximation49
   b. Thing
   c. Undefined
   d. Undefined

50. An _____ is a straight line or curve A to which another curve B approaches closer and closer as one moves along it. As one moves along B, the space between it and the _____ A becomes smaller and smaller, and can in fact be made as small as one could wish by going far enough along. A curve may or may not touch or cross its _____. In fact, the curve may intersect the _____ an infinite number of times.
   a. Thing
   b. Asymptote50
   c. Undefined
   d. Undefined

51. In astronomy, geography, geometry and related sciences and contexts, a plane is said to be _____ at a given point if it is locally perpendicular to the gradient of the gravity field, i.e., with the direction of the gravitational force at that point.

Chapter 4. Polynomial and Rational Functions

a. Thing
b. Horizontal51
c. Undefined
d. Undefined

52. In mathematics, a _____ is any function which can be written as the ratio of two polynomial functions.
a. Thing
b. Rational function52
c. Undefined
d. Undefined

53. _____ is a straight line or curve A to which another curve B the one being studied approaches closer and closer as one moves along it.
a. Vertical asymptote53
b. Thing
c. Undefined
d. Undefined

54. In sociology and biology a _____ is the collection of people or organisms of a particular species living in a given geographic area or space, usually measured by a census.
a. Thing
b. Population54
c. Undefined
d. Undefined

55. _____ is mass m per unit volume V.
a. Density55
b. Thing
c. Undefined
d. Undefined

56. In economics, business, and accounting, a _____ is the value of money that has been used up to produce something, and hence is not available for use anymore. In business, the _____ may be one of acquisition, in which case the amount of money expended to acquire it is counted as _____.

Chapter 4. Polynomial and Rational Functions

a. Thing
b. Cost56
c. Undefined
d. Undefined

57. _____ is the largest positive integer that divides both numbers without remainder.
   a. Common factor57
   b. Thing
   c. Undefined
   d. Undefined

58. A _____ represents a system whose behavior is not expressible as a sum of the behaviors of its descriptors.
   a. Thing
   b. Nonlinear system58
   c. Undefined
   d. Undefined

59. In geometry, an _____ angle is an angle that is not a 90 degree angle, or an angle that is divisible by 90: 180, 270, 360/0
   a. Thing
   b. Oblique59
   c. Undefined
   d. Undefined

60. Continuous functions are of utmost importance in mathematics and applications. However, not all functions are continuous. If a function is not continuous at a point in its domain, one says that it has a _____ there. The set of all points of _____ of a function may be a discrete set, a dense set, or even the entire domain of the function.
   a. Discontinuity60
   b. Thing
   c. Undefined
   d. Undefined

61. An _____ is a mathematical statement, in symbols, that two things are the same or equivalent. Equations are written with an equal sign, as in 2 + 3 = 5.

a. Equation61
b. Thing
c. Undefined
d. Undefined

62. _____ systems represent systems whose behavior is not expressible as a sum of the behaviors of its descriptors.
a. Nonlinear62
b. Thing
c. Undefined
d. Undefined

63. _____ are a set of equations containing multiple variables.
a. Systems of equations63
b. Thing
c. Undefined
d. Undefined

64. A _____ is one of the basic shapes of geometry: a polygon with three vertices and three sides which are straight line segments.
a. Triangle64
b. Thing
c. Undefined
d. Undefined

65. In mathematics, a _____ is a quadric surface, with the following equation in Cartesian coordinates: $(x/a)^2 + (y/b)^2 = 1$.
a. Cylinder65
b. Thing
c. Undefined
d. Undefined

66. In mathematics, specifically in topology, a _____ is a two-dimensional manifold. The most familiar examples are those that arise as the boundaries of solid objects in ordinary three-dimensional Euclidean space, E^3.

a. Surface66
b. Thing
c. Undefined
d. Undefined

67. In mathematics, a _____ is a polynomial equation of the third degree.
a. Thing
b. Cubic equation67
c. Undefined
d. Undefined

68. _____ of a polynomial with real or complex coefficients is a certain expression in the coefficients of the polynomial which is equal to zero if and only if the polynomial has a multiple root i.e. a root with multiplicity greater than one in the complex numbers.
a. Discriminant68
b. Thing
c. Undefined
d. Undefined

69. A _____ is a set of numbers that designate location in a given reference system, such as x,y in a planar _____ system or an x,y,z in a three-dimensional _____ system.
a. Thing
b. Coordinate69
c. Undefined
d. Undefined

70. A _____ signifies a point or points of probability on a subject e.g., the _____ of creativity, which allows for the formation of rule or norm or law by interpretation of the phenomena events that can be created.
a. Thing
b. Principle70
c. Undefined
d. Undefined

Chapter 5. Exponential and Logarithmic Functions

1. _____ refers to selected population characteristics as used in government, marketing or opinion research, or the demographic profiles used in such research.
   a. Demographics1
   b. Thing
   c. Undefined
   d. Undefined

2. In mathematics, _____ growth occurs when the growth rate of a function is always proportional to the function's current size.
   a. Thing
   b. Exponential2
   c. Undefined
   d. Undefined

3. _____ is one of the most important functions in mathematics. A function commonly used to study growth and decay
   a. Exponential function3
   b. Thing
   c. Undefined
   d. Undefined

4. The mathematical concept of a _____ expresses the intuitive idea of deterministic dependence between two quantities, one of which is viewed as primary and the other as secondary. A _____ then is a way to associate a unique output for each input of a specified type, for example, a real number or an element of a given set.
   a. Thing
   b. Function4
   c. Undefined
   d. Undefined

5. _____ has many meanings, most of which simply .
   a. Power5
   b. Thing
   c. Undefined
   d. Undefined

6. _____ are the basic objects of study in graph theory. Informally speaking, a graph is a set of objects called points, nodes, or vertices connected by links called lines or edges.

a. Graphs6
b. Thing
c. Undefined
d. Undefined

7. A _____ is a polynomial function of the form $f(x) = ax^2 + bx + c$, where a, b, c are real numbers and a , 0.
a. Quadratic function7
b. Event
c. Undefined
d. Undefined

8. In philosophy, mathematics, and logic, a _____ is an attribute of an object; thus a red object is said to have the _____ of redness.
a. Thing
b. Property8
c. Undefined
d. Undefined

9. _____ interest refers to the fact that whenever interest is calculated, it is based not only on the original principal, but also on any unpaid interest that has been added to the principal.
a. Compound9
b. Thing
c. Undefined
d. Undefined

10. _____ refers to the fact that whenever interest is calculated, it is based not only on the original principal, but also on any unpaid interest that has been added to the principal. The more frequently interest is compounded, the faster the balance grows.
a. Compound interest10
b. Concept
c. Undefined
d. Undefined

11. In mathematics and in the sciences, a _____ is a concise way of expressing information symbolically or a general relationship between quantities.

a. Formula11
b. Thing
c. Undefined
d. Undefined

12. _____ is the fee paid on borrowed money.
a. Thing
b. Interest12
c. Undefined
d. Undefined

13. A _____ typically refers to a class of handheld calculators that are capable of plotting graphs, solving equation systems, and performing numerous other tasks with variables.
a. Thing
b. Graphing calculator13
c. Undefined
d. Undefined

14. In sociology and biology a _____ is the collection of people or organisms of a particular species living in a given geographic area or space, usually measured by a census.
a. Population14
b. Thing
c. Undefined
d. Undefined

15. The _____ of a quantity, subject to exponential decay, is the time required for the quantity to decay to half of its initial value. The concept originated in the study of radioactive decay, but applies to many other fields as well, including phenomena which are described by non-exponential decays.
a. Half-life15
b. Thing
c. Undefined
d. Undefined

16. _____ is the process in which an unstable atomic nucleus loses energy by emitting radiation in the form of particles or electromagnetic waves.

Chapter 5. Exponential and Logarithmic Functions

   a. Thing
   b. Radioactive decay16
   c. Undefined
   d. Undefined

17. John _____ of Merchistoun , nicknamed Marvellous Merchistoun, was a Scottish mathematician, physicist, astronomer/astrologer and 8th Laird of Merchistoun. He is most remembered as the inventor of logarithms and _____'s bones, and for popularizing the use of the decimal point.
   a. Person
   b. Napier17
   c. Undefined
   d. Undefined

18. In mathematics, a _____ number is a real or complex number which is not algebraic, that is, not a solution of a non-zero polynomial equation, with rational coefficients.
   a. Transcendental18
   b. Thing
   c. Undefined
   d. Undefined

19. _____ element of an element x with respect to a binary operation * with identity element e is an element y such that x * y = y * x = e. In particular,
   a. Inverse19
   b. Thing
   c. Undefined
   d. Undefined

20. An _____ is a function which does the reverse of a given function.
   a. Thing
   b. Inverse function20
   c. Undefined
   d. Undefined

21. A _____ of a number is a number a such that $a^3 = x$.

Chapter 5. Exponential and Logarithmic Functions

    a. Thing
    b. Cube root21
    c. Undefined
    d. Undefined

22. In mathematics, a _____ of a number x is the exponent y of the power by such that $x = b^y$. The value used for the base b must be neither 0 nor 1, nor a root of 1 in the case of the extension to complex numbers, and is typically 10, e, or 2.
    a. Thing
    b. Logarithm22
    c. Undefined
    d. Undefined

23. Mathematical _____ is used in mathematics, and throughout the physical sciences, engineering, and economics. The complexity of such _____ ranges from relatively simple symbolic representations, such as numbers 1 and 2; function symbols sin and +, to conceptual symbols, such as lim and dy/dx; to equations and variables.
    a. Notation23
    b. Thing
    c. Undefined
    d. Undefined

24. In mathematics, a _____ of a complex-valued function f is a member x of the domain of f such that f(x) vanishes at x, that is, x : f (x) = 0.
    a. Thing
    b. Root24
    c. Undefined
    d. Undefined

25. In plane geometry, a _____ is a polygon with four equal sides, four right angles, and parallel opposite sides. In algebra, the _____ of a number is that number multiplied by itself.
    a. Square25
    b. Thing
    c. Undefined
    d. Undefined

26. In mathematics, the _____ is the logarithm with base 10.

Chapter 5. Exponential and Logarithmic Functions

   a. Thing
   b. Common logarithm26
   c. Undefined
   d. Undefined

27. An _____ is the result from the sudden release of stored energy in the Earth's crust that creates seismic waves.
   a. Earthquake27
   b. Thing
   c. Undefined
   d. Undefined

28. The _____ of a mathematical object is its size: a property by which it can be larger or smaller than other objects of the same kind; in technical terms, an ordering of the class of objects to which it belongs.
   a. Thing
   b. Magnitude28
   c. Undefined
   d. Undefined

29. A frame of _____ is a particular perspective from which the universe is observed.
   a. Thing
   b. Reference29
   c. Undefined
   d. Undefined

30. _____ commonly refers to the 'output' of a function.
   a. Thing
   b. Value30
   c. Undefined
   d. Undefined

31. _____ is a mathematical operation, written a^n, involving two numbers, the base a and the exponent n.

a. Exponentiating31
b. Thing
c. Undefined
d. Undefined

32. _____ is a measure of the acidity or alkalinity of a solution.
a. Thing
b. PH level32
c. Undefined
d. Undefined

33. In _____ algebra, a *-ring is an associative ring with an antilinear, antiautomorphism * : A ¨ A which is an involution.
a. Thing
b. Star33
c. Undefined
d. Undefined

34. In arithmetic, the _____ refers to the number b in an expression of the form b^n.
a. Base34
b. Thing
c. Undefined
d. Undefined

35. In geometry, an _____ of a triangle is a straight line through a vertex and perpendicular to (i.e. forming a right angle with) the opposite side or an extension of the opposite side.
a. Altitude35
b. Concept
c. Undefined
d. Undefined

36. _____ is a term used in accounting, economics and finance with reference to the fact that assets with finite lives lose value over time.

Chapter 5. Exponential and Logarithmic Functions

a. Depreciation36
b. Thing
c. Undefined
d. Undefined

37. An _____ is a mathematical statement, in symbols, that two things are the same or equivalent. Equations are written with an equal sign, as in 2 + 3 = 5.
a. Equation37
b. Thing
c. Undefined
d. Undefined

38. _____ variables are variables other than the independent variable that may bear any effect on the behavior of the subject being studied.
a. Thing
b. Extraneous38
c. Undefined
d. Undefined

39. _____ states that the rate of heat loss of a body is proportional to the difference in temperatures between the body and its surroundings.
a. Thing
b. Newton's law of cooling39
c. Undefined
d. Undefined

40. An _____ is the fee paid on borrow money.
a. Concept
b. Interest rate40
c. Undefined
d. Undefined

41. A _____ is a special kind of ratio, indicating a relationship between two measurements with different units, such as miles to gallons or cents to pounds.

Chapter 5. Exponential and Logarithmic Functions

a. Thing
b. Rate41
c. Undefined
d. Undefined

42. _____ of a single or multiple future payments is the nominal amounts of money to change hands at some future date, discounted to account for the time value of money, and other factors such as investment risk.
a. Present value42
b. Thing
c. Undefined
d. Undefined

43. The word _____ comes from the Latin word linearis, which means created by lines.
a. Thing
b. Linear43
c. Undefined
d. Undefined

44. A _____ is an equation in which each term is either a constant or the product of a constant times the first power of a variable.
a. Thing
b. Linear equation44
c. Undefined
d. Undefined

45. _____ systems represent systems whose behavior is not expressible as a sum of the behaviors of its descriptors.
a. Thing
b. Nonlinear45
c. Undefined
d. Undefined

46. A _____ is a symbolic representation denoting a quantity or expression. It often represents an "unknown" quantity that has the potential to change.

Chapter 5. Exponential and Logarithmic Functions

a. Thing
b. Variable46
c. Undefined
d. Undefined

47. _____ is a decrease that follows an exponential function.
a. Exponential decay47
b. Thing
c. Undefined
d. Undefined

48. In mathematics, _____ occurs when the growth rate of a function is always proportional to the function's current size.
a. Thing
b. Exponential growth48
c. Undefined
d. Undefined

49. _____ is the distribution of a single lump-sum cash flow into many smaller cash flow installments, as determined by an _____ schedule.
a. Amortization49
b. Thing
c. Undefined
d. Undefined

50. _____ measures the nominal future sum of money that a given sum of money is "worth" at a specified time in the future assuming a certain interest rate; this value does not include corrections for inflation or other factors that affect the true value of money in the future.
a. Future value50
b. Thing
c. Undefined
d. Undefined

51. _____ is a part of mathematics concerned with questions of size, shape, and relative position of figures and with properties of space.

a. Geometry51
b. Thing
c. Undefined
d. Undefined

52. A _____ is a sequence of numbers where each term after the first is found by multiplying the previous one by a fixed non-zero number called the common ratio.
   a. Geometric sequence52
   b. Thing
   c. Undefined
   d. Undefined

53. In mathematics, a _____ is an ordered list of objects. Like a set, it contains members, also called elements or terms, and the number of terms is called the length of the _____. Unlike a set, order matters, and the exact same elements can appear multiple times at different positions in the _____.
   a. Thing
   b. Sequence53
   c. Undefined
   d. Undefined

54. _____ was a device used in Great Britain in the 18th century to reduce national debt.
   a. Sinking fund54
   b. Thing
   c. Undefined
   d. Undefined

55. A _____ is a method of using property as security for the payment of a debt.
   a. Thing
   b. Mortgage55
   c. Undefined
   d. Undefined

56. _____ is a kind of property which exists as magnitude or multitude. It is among the basic classes of things along with quality, substance, change, and relation.

Chapter 5. Exponential and Logarithmic Functions

   a. Amount56
   b. Thing
   c. Undefined
   d. Undefined

57. _____ is a synonym for information.
   a. Data57
   b. Thing
   c. Undefined
   d. Undefined

58. In mathematics, a _____ can be thought of as any collection of distinct objects considered as a whole.
   a. Thing
   b. Set58
   c. Undefined
   d. Undefined

59. In mathematics, a _____ set is the complement of a meager set. A meager set is one which is the countable union of nowhere dense sets.
   a. Residual59
   b. Thing
   c. Undefined
   d. Undefined

60. In mathematics, _____ is the process of constructing new data points outside a discrete set of known data points. It is similar to the process of interpolation, which constructs new points between known points, but its results are often less meaningful, and are subject to greater uncertainty.
   a. Thing
   b. Extrapolation60
   c. Undefined
   d. Undefined

61. _____ is a method of constructing new data points from a discrete set of known data points.

a. Thing
b. Interpolation61
c. Undefined
d. Undefined

62. _____ usually refers to the biological _____ of a population level that can be supported for an organism, given the quantity of food, habitat, water and other life infrastructure present.
a. Carrying capacity62
b. Thing
c. Undefined
d. Undefined

63. _____ is the ability to hold, receive or absorb, or a measure thereof, similar to the concept of volume.
a. Concept
b. Capacity63
c. Undefined
d. Undefined

64. The _____ refers to a relationship between the duration of learning or experience and the resulting progress
a. Learning curve64
b. Thing
c. Undefined
d. Undefined

Chapter 6. Systems of Equations and Inequalities

1. In mathematics, _____ problems involve the optimization of a linear objective function, subject to linear equality and inequality constraints.
    a. Thing
    b. Linear programming1
    c. Undefined
    d. Undefined

2. The word _____ comes from the Latin word linearis, which means created by lines.
    a. Thing
    b. Linear2
    c. Undefined
    d. Undefined

3. _____ is the property of two events happening at the same time in at least one reference frame.
    a. Thing
    b. Simultaneous3
    c. Undefined
    d. Undefined

4. In mathematics, a _____ is a number, function, or distribution which satisfies an equation.
    a. Solution4
    b. Thing
    c. Undefined
    d. Undefined

5. An _____ is a mathematical statement, in symbols, that two things are the same or equivalent. Equations are written with an equal sign, as in 2 + 3 = 5.
    a. Thing
    b. Equation5
    c. Undefined
    d. Undefined

6. A _____ is an equation in which each term is either a constant or the product of a constant times the first power of a variable.

a. Linear equation6
b. Thing
c. Undefined
d. Undefined

7. A _____ is a symbolic representation denoting a quantity or expression. It often represents an "unknown" quantity that has the potential to change.
a. Thing
b. Variable7
c. Undefined
d. Undefined

8. _____ are a set of equations containing multiple variables.
a. Systems of equations8
b. Thing
c. Undefined
d. Undefined

9. The mathematical concept of a _____ expresses the intuitive idea of deterministic dependence between two quantities, one of which is viewed as primary and the other as secondary. A _____ then is a way to associate a unique output for each input of a specified type, for example, a real number or an element of a given set.
a. Function9
b. Thing
c. Undefined
d. Undefined

10. Equivalence is the condition of being _____ or essentially equal.
a. Thing
b. Equivalent10
c. Undefined
d. Undefined

11. A _____ can be described as an infinitely thin, infinitely long, perfectly straight curve containing an infinite number of points.

a. Line11
b. Thing
c. Undefined
d. Undefined

12. _____ is the estimation of a physical quantity such as distance, energy, temperature, or time.
a. Thing
b. Measurement12
c. Undefined
d. Undefined

13. _____ is a physical property of a system that underlies the common notions of hot and cold; something that is hotter has the greater _____.
a. Thing
b. Temperature13
c. Undefined
d. Undefined

14. An _____ is a straight line around which a geometric figure can be rotated.
a. Axis14
b. Thing
c. Undefined
d. Undefined

15. _____ are the basic objects of study in graph theory. Informally speaking, a graph is a set of objects called points, nodes, or vertices connected by links called lines or edges.
a. Graphs 15
b. Thing
c. Undefined
d. Undefined

16. _____ is a set, with some particular properties and usually some additional structure, such as the operations of addition or multiplication, for instance.

Chapter 6. Systems of Equations and Inequalities

a. Space16
b. Thing
c. Undefined
d. Undefined

17. In mathematics, a _____ is an n-tuple with n being 3.
a. Thing
b. Triple17
c. Undefined
d. Undefined

18. A _____ is the quantity that defines certain relatively constant characteristics of systems or functions..
a. Parameter18
b. Thing
c. Undefined
d. Undefined

19. In plane geometry, a _____ is a polygon with four equal sides, four right angles, and parallel opposite sides. In algebra, the _____ of a number is that number multiplied by itself.
a. Thing
b. Square19
c. Undefined
d. Undefined

20. In common usage, a _____ is a parameter or measurement required to define the characteristics of an object-"i.e. length, width, and height or size and shape. In mathematics, they are the parameters required to describe the position and relevant characteristics of any object within a conceptual space.
a. Dimension20
b. Thing
c. Undefined
d. Undefined

21. In neutral geometry, the minimum _____ between two points is the length of the line segment between them.

Chapter 6. Systems of Equations and Inequalities

a. Thing
b. Distance21
c. Undefined
d. Undefined

22. In mathematics, _____ geometry was the traditional name for the geometry of three-dimensional Euclidean space — for practical purposes the kind of space we live in.
a. Solid22
b. Thing
c. Undefined
d. Undefined

23. Leonhard _____ was a pioneering Swiss mathematician and physicist, who spent most of his life in Russia and Germany.
a. Euler23
b. Person
c. Undefined
d. Undefined

24. _____ was a pioneering Swiss mathematician and physicist, who spent most of his life in Russia and Germany
a. Person
b. Euler Leonhard24
c. Undefined
d. Undefined

25. _____ is either of the two parts into which a plane divides the three-dimensional space. More generally, a _____ is either of the two parts into which a hyperplane divides an affine space.
a. Thing
b. Half-space25
c. Undefined
d. Undefined

26. A _____ is a set of possible values that a variable can take on in order to satisfy a given set of conditions, which may include equations and inequalities.

Chapter 6. Systems of Equations and Inequalities

a. Solution set26
b. Thing
c. Undefined
d. Undefined

27. _____ are illustrations used in the branch of mathematics known as set theory. They show all of the possible mathematical or logical relationships between sets (groups of things).
a. Thing
b. Venn diagrams27
c. Undefined
d. Undefined

28. A _____ is a simplified and structured visual representation of concepts, ideas, constructions, relations, statistical data, anatomy etc used in all aspects of human activities to visualize and clarify the topic.
a. Diagram28
b. Thing
c. Undefined
d. Undefined

29. In mathematics, _____ are two-dimensional manifolds or surfaces that are perfectly flat.
a. Planes29
b. Thing
c. Undefined
d. Undefined

30. In mathematics, a _____ can be thought of as any collection of distinct objects considered as a whole.
a. Thing
b. Set30
c. Undefined
d. Undefined

31. An _____ is any starting assumption from which other statements are logically derived

Chapter 6. Systems of Equations and Inequalities

a. Axiom31
b. Thing
c. Undefined
d. Undefined

32. In optimization, a candidate solution is a member of a set of possible solutions to a given problem. A candidate solution does not have to be a likely or reasonable solution to the problem. The space of all candidate solutions is called the _____, feasible set, search space, or solution space.
   a. Thing
   b. Feasible region32
   c. Undefined
   d. Undefined

33. _____ commonly refers to the 'output' of a function.
   a. Value33
   b. Thing
   c. Undefined
   d. Undefined

34. A _____ signifies a point or points of probability on a subject e.g., the _____ of creativity, which allows for the formation of rule or norm or law by interpretation of the phenomena events that can be created.
   a. Thing
   b. Principle34
   c. Undefined
   d. Undefined

35. In mathematics, a _____ is a condition that a solution to an optimization problem must satisfy in order to be acceptable.
   a. Constraint35
   b. Thing
   c. Undefined
   d. Undefined

36. A _____ typically refers to a class of handheld calculators that are capable of plotting graphs, solving equation systems, and performing numerous other tasks with variables.

Chapter 6. Systems of Equations and Inequalities

   a. Thing
   b. Graphing calculator36
   c. Undefined
   d. Undefined

37. _____ is a physical quantity expressing the size of a part of a surface. The term can also be used in a non-mathematical context to be mean "vicinity".
   a. Thing
   b. Area37
   c. Undefined
   d. Undefined

38. The _____ of a solid object is the three-dimensional concept of how much space it occupies, often quantified numerically.
   a. Thing
   b. Volume38
   c. Undefined
   d. Undefined

39. In mathematics, the _____ (or modulus) of a real number is its numerical value without regard to its sign.
   a. Thing
   b. Absolute value39
   c. Undefined
   d. Undefined

40. A _____ is any value or expression separated from another _____ by a + or - sign in an overall expression.
   a. Term40
   b. Thing
   c. Undefined
   d. Undefined

41. A _____ function is a function for which, intuitively, small changes in the input result in small changes in the output.

Chapter 6. Systems of Equations and Inequalities

   a. Continuous41
   b. Event
   c. Undefined
   d. Undefined

42. In mathematics, two sets are said to be _____ if they have no element in common. For example, {1, 2, 3} and {4, 5, 6} are sets which are _____.
   a. Thing
   b. Disjoint42
   c. Undefined
   d. Undefined

43. In elementary algebra, an _____ is a set that contains every real number between two indicated numbers and may contain the two numbers themselves.
   a. Thing
   b. Interval43
   c. Undefined
   d. Undefined

44. In mathematics, an inequality is a statement about the relative size or order of two objects. For example 9 < 10, or 9 is _____ 10.
   a. Thing
   b. Less than44
   c. Undefined
   d. Undefined

45. In mathematics, an inequality is a statement about the relative size or order of two objects. For example 14 > 10, or 14 is _____ 10.
   a. Greater than45
   b. Thing
   c. Undefined
   d. Undefined

46. In mathematics, a _____ is a rectangular table of numbers or, more generally, a table consisting of abstract quantities that can be added and multiplied.

Chapter 6. Systems of Equations and Inequalities

a. Thing
b. Matrix46
c. Undefined
d. Undefined

47. In linear algebra, the _____ of a matrix is obtained by combining two matrices in such a way that a matrix of coefficients to which has been added a column of constants corresponds to the right hand side of the equations.
a. Augmented matrix47
b. Thing
c. Undefined
d. Undefined

48. In mathematics, a _____ is a constant multiplicative factor of a certain object. The object can be such things as a variable, a vector, a function, etc. For example, the _____ of $9x^2$ is 9.
a. Coefficient48
b. Thing
c. Undefined
d. Undefined

49. In mathematics and the mathematical sciences, a _____ is a fixed, but possibly unspecified, value. This is in contrast to a variable, which is not fixed.
a. Thing
b. Constant49
c. Undefined
d. Undefined

50. _____ are elementary linear transformations on a matrix which preserve matrix equivalence.
a. Thing
b. Elementary row operations50
c. Undefined
d. Undefined

51. Elementary _____ are simple transformations which can be applied to a matrix without changing the linear system of equations that it represents.

Chapter 6. Systems of Equations and Inequalities

a. Thing
b. Row operations51
c. Undefined
d. Undefined

52. _____ is a special kind of square matrix where the entries below or above the main diagonal are zero.
a. Thing
b. Triangular form52
c. Undefined
d. Undefined

53. In linear algebra, Gauss–Jordan elimination is a version of Gaussian elimination that puts zeros both above and below each pivot element as it goes from the top row of the given matrix to the bottom. In other words, _____ elimination brings a matrix to reduced row echelon form, whereas Gaussian elimination takes it only as far as row echelon form.
a. Thing
b. Gauss-Jordan53
c. Undefined
d. Undefined

54. _____ is a version of Gaussian elimination that puts zeros both above and below each pivot element as it goes from the top row of the given matrix to the bottom.
a. Thing
b. Gauss-Jordan elimination54
c. Undefined
d. Undefined

55. _____ is an algorithm which can be used to determine the solutions of a system of linear equations, to find the rank of a matrix, and to calculate the inverse of an invertible square matrix.
a. Thing
b. Gaussian elimination55
c. Undefined
d. Undefined

Chapter 6. Systems of Equations and Inequalities

56. In mathematics, a matrix is in _____ form, also known as row canonical form - the resulting matrix is sometimes called a Hermite matrix; if it satisfies the following requirements: All nonzero rows are above any rows of all zeroes, The leading coefficient of a row is always to the right of the leading coefficient of the row above it, All leading coefficients are 1, and All entries above a leading coefficient in the same column are zero.
   a. Reduced row-echelon56
   b. Thing
   c. Undefined
   d. Undefined

57. In mathematics, a matrix is in _____ if is satisfies the following requirements. All nonzero rows are above any rows of all zeroes. The leading coefficient of a row is always strictly to the right of the leading coefficient of the row above it.
   a. Row-echelon form57
   b. Thing
   c. Undefined
   d. Undefined

58. A _____ is one of the basic shapes of geometry: a polygon with three vertices and three sides which are straight line segments.
   a. Thing
   b. Triangle58
   c. Undefined
   d. Undefined

59. Two mathematical objects are equal if and only if they are precisely the same in every way. This defines a binary relation, _____, denoted by the sign of _____ "=" in such a way that the statement "x = y" means that x and y are equal.
   a. Thing
   b. Equality59
   c. Undefined
   d. Undefined

60. _____ is the mathematical operation of combining or adding two numbers to obtain an equal simple amount or total.

Chapter 6. Systems of Equations and Inequalities

   a. Thing
   b. Addition60
   c. Undefined
   d. Undefined

61. _____ is one of the four basic arithmetic operations; it is essentially the opposite of addition.
   a. Thing
   b. Subtraction61
   c. Undefined
   d. Undefined

62. In mathematics, the _____ inverse, or opposite, of a number n is the number that, when added to n, yields zero. The _____ inverse of n is denoted −n.
   a. Thing
   b. Additive62
   c. Undefined
   d. Undefined

63. In mathematics the _____ of a set which is equipped with the operation of addition is an element which, when added to any other element x in the set, yields x.
   a. Additive identity63
   b. Concept
   c. Undefined
   d. Undefined

64. In mathematics, the _____ of a number n is the number that, when added to n, yields zero. The _____ of n is denoted −n. For example, 7 is −7, because 7 + (−7) = 0, and the _____ of −0.3 is 0.3, because −0.3 + 0.3 = 0.
   a. Additive inverse64
   b. Thing
   c. Undefined
   d. Undefined

65. In linear algebra, real numbers are called scalars and relate to vectors in a vector space through the operation of _____ multiplication, in which a vector can be multiplied by a number to produce another vector.

a. Thing
b. Scalar65
c. Undefined
d. Undefined

66. _____ is one of the basic operations defining a vector space in linear algebra.
a. Scalar multiplication66
b. Thing
c. Undefined
d. Undefined

67. An _____ is an equality that remains true regardless of the values of any variables that appear within it, to distinguish it from an equality which is true under more particular conditions.
a. Thing
b. Identity67
c. Undefined
d. Undefined

68. _____ element of an element x with respect to a binary operation * with identity element e is an element y such that x * y = y * x = e. In particular,
a. Inverse68
b. Thing
c. Undefined
d. Undefined

69. In mathematics, _____ is an elementary arithmetic operation. When one of the numbers is a whole number, _____ is the repeated sum of the other number.
a. Multiplication69
b. Thing
c. Undefined
d. Undefined

70. _____ is the distance around a given two-dimensional object. As a general rule, the _____ of a polygon can always be calculated by adding all the length of the sides together. So, the formula for triangles is P = a + b + c, where a, b and c stand for each side of it. For quadrilaterals the equation is P = a + b + c + d. For equilateral polygons, P = na, where n is the number of sides and a is the side length.

a. Thing
b. Perimeter70
c. Undefined
d. Undefined

71. In geometry, a _____ is defined as a quadrilateral where all four of its angles are right angles.
a. Rectangle71
b. Thing
c. Undefined
d. Undefined

72. In algebra, a _____ is a function depending on n that associates a scalar, det(A), to every $n \times n$ square matrix A.
a. Thing
b. Determinant72
c. Undefined
d. Undefined

73. In linear algebra, a _____ of a matrix A is the determinant of some smaller square matrix, cut down from A.
a. Thing
b. Minor73
c. Undefined
d. Undefined

74. An _____ of a product of sums expresses it as a sum of products by using the fact that multiplication distributes over addition.
a. Thing
b. Expansion74
c. Undefined
d. Undefined

75. _____ is a theorem in linear algebra, which gives the solution of a system of linear equations in terms of determinants.

Chapter 6. Systems of Equations and Inequalities

   a. Cramer's Rule75
   b. Thing
   c. Undefined
   d. Undefined

76. Three or more points that lie on the same line are called _____.
   a. Collinear76
   b. Thing
   c. Undefined
   d. Undefined

77. In three or more dimensions, lines may also be skew, meaning they don't meet, but also don't define a plane. Two distinct planes intersect in at most one line. Three or more points that lie on the same line are called _____.
   a. Collinear points77
   b. Concept
   c. Undefined
   d. Undefined

78. In algebra, the _____ decomposition or _____ expansion is used to reduce the degree of either the numerator or the denominator of a rational function.
   a. Thing
   b. Partial fraction78
   c. Undefined
   d. Undefined

79. Acid _____ ratio measures the ability of a company to use its near cash or quick assets to immediately extinguish its current liabilities.
   a. Test79
   b. Thing
   c. Undefined
   d. Undefined

80. In mathematics, a _____ is a way of expressing a number of equal parts. A _____ consists of two numbers, a numerator which gives the number of equal parts and a denominator which gives the number of those parts that make up a whole.

Chapter 6. Systems of Equations and Inequalities

  a. Fraction80
  b. Thing
  c. Undefined
  d. Undefined

81. A spatial _____ is a concept used to define an exact location in space. It has no volume, area or length.
  a. Point81
  b. Thing
  c. Undefined
  d. Undefined

82. An _____ is a combination of numbers, operators, grouping symbols and/or free variables and bound variables arranged in a meaningful way which can be evaluated..
  a. Thing
  b. Expression82
  c. Undefined
  d. Undefined

83. In mathematics, a _____ number is a number which can be expressed as a ratio of two integers. Non-integer _____ numbers (commonly called fractions) are usually written as the vulgar fraction a / b, where b is not zero.
  a. Rational83
  b. Thing
  c. Undefined
  d. Undefined

Chapter 7. Conic Sections and Non-Linear Systems

1. In mathematics, a _____ section is a curve that can be formed by intersecting a cone with a plane.
   a. Conic1
   b. Thing
   c. Undefined
   d. Undefined

2. In mathematics, a _____ is a curve that can be formed by intersecting a cone with a plane.
   a. Conic section2
   b. Thing
   c. Undefined
   d. Undefined

3. In geometry, a _____ is a special kind of point, usually a corner of a polygon, polyhedron, or higher dimensional polytope. In the geometry of curves a _____ is a point of where the first derivative of curvature is zero. In graph theory, a _____ is the fundamental unit out of which graphs are formed
   a. Thing
   b. Vertex3
   c. Undefined
   d. Undefined

4. In geometry, the _____ of an object is a point in some sense in the middle of the object.
   a. Thing
   b. Center4
   c. Undefined
   d. Undefined

5. In classical geometry, a _____ of a circle or sphere is any line segment from its center to its boundary. By extension, the _____ of a circle or sphere is the length of any such segment. The _____ is half the diameter. In science and engineering the term _____ of curvature is commonly used as a synonym for _____.
   a. Radius5
   b. Thing
   c. Undefined
   d. Undefined

6. _____ is a three-dimensional geometric shape formed by straight lines through a fixed point vertex to the points of a fixed curve directrix.

a. Right circular cone6
b. Thing
c. Undefined
d. Undefined

7. In Euclidean geometry, a _____ is the set of all points in a plane at a fixed distance, called the radius, from a given point, the center.
a. Thing
b. Circle7
c. Undefined
d. Undefined

8. A _____ is a three-dimensional geometric shape formed by straight lines through a fixed point (vertex) to the points of a fixed curve (directrix)
a. Cone8
b. Concept
c. Undefined
d. Undefined

9. An _____ is a mathematical statement, in symbols, that two things are the same or equivalent. Equations are written with an equal sign, as in 2 + 3 = 5.
a. Thing
b. Equation9
c. Undefined
d. Undefined

10. In mathematics, a _____ case is a limiting case in which a class of object changes its nature so as to belong to another, usually simpler, class.
a. Thing
b. Degenerate10
c. Undefined
d. Undefined

11. In mathematics, _____ is a limiting case in which a class of object changes its nature so as to belong to another, usually simpler, class.

a. Degeneracy11
b. Thing
c. Undefined
d. Undefined

12. In mathematics, a _____ is an expression that is constructed from one or more variables and constants, using only the operations of addition, subtraction, multiplication, and constant positive whole number exponents. is a _____. Note in particular that division by an expression containing a variable is not in general allowed in polynomials.
   a. Polynomial12
   b. Thing
   c. Undefined
   d. Undefined

13. In mathematics, an _____ .
   a. Ellipse13
   b. Thing
   c. Undefined
   d. Undefined

14. _____ is a notation for writing numbers that is often used by scientists and mathematicians to make it easier to write large and small numbers.
   a. Scientific notation14
   b. Thing
   c. Undefined
   d. Undefined

15. A _____ typically refers to a class of handheld calculators that are capable of plotting graphs, solving equation systems, and performing numerous other tasks with variables.
   a. Graphing calculator15
   b. Thing
   c. Undefined
   d. Undefined

16. _____ is a physical quantity expressing the size of a part of a surface. The term can also be used in a non-mathematical context to be mean "vicinity".

Chapter 7. Conic Sections and Non-Linear Systems

a. Area16
b. Thing
c. Undefined
d. Undefined

17. In plane geometry, a _____ is a polygon with four equal sides, four right angles, and parallel opposite sides. In algebra, the _____ of a number is that number multiplied by itself.
    a. Square17
    b. Thing
    c. Undefined
    d. Undefined

18. In mathematics, a _____ is a type of conic section defined as the intersection between a right circular conical surface and a plane which cuts through both halves of the cone.
    a. Hyperbola18
    b. Thing
    c. Undefined
    d. Undefined

19. In mathematics, the _____ (or modulus) of a real number is its numerical value without regard to its sign.
    a. Absolute value19
    b. Thing
    c. Undefined
    d. Undefined

20. The mathematical concept of a _____ expresses the intuitive idea of deterministic dependence between two quantities, one of which is viewed as primary and the other as secondary. A _____ then is a way to associate a unique output for each input of a specified type, for example, a real number or an element of a given set.
    a. Thing
    b. Function20
    c. Undefined
    d. Undefined

21. _____ commonly refers to the 'output' of a function.

a. Thing
b. Value21
c. Undefined
d. Undefined

22. _____ is a technique used in algebra to solve quadratic equations, in analytic geometry for determining the shapes of graphs, and in calculus for computing integrals, including, but hardly limited to, the integrals that define Laplace transforms. The essential objective is to reduce a quadratic polynomial in a variable in an equation or expression to a squared polynomial of linear order. This can reduce an equation or integral to one that is more easily solved or evaluated.
    a. Thing
    b. Completing the square22
    c. Undefined
    d. Undefined

23. _____ systems represent systems whose behavior is not expressible as a sum of the behaviors of its descriptors.
    a. Thing
    b. Nonlinear23
    c. Undefined
    d. Undefined

24. A _____ represents a system whose behavior is not expressible as a sum of the behaviors of its descriptors.
    a. Nonlinear system24
    b. Thing
    c. Undefined
    d. Undefined

25. In mathematics, a _____ is a number, function, or distribution which satisfies an equation.
    a. Solution25
    b. Thing
    c. Undefined
    d. Undefined

26. In economics, supply and _____ describe market relations between prospective sellers and buyers of a good.

Chapter 7. Conic Sections and Non-Linear Systems

a. Demand26
b. Thing
c. Undefined
d. Undefined

27. _____ can be defined as the graph depicting the relationship between the price of a certain commodity, and the amount of it that consumers are willing and able to purchase at that given price demand.
a. Demand curve27
b. Thing
c. Undefined
d. Undefined

28. In economics, economic equilibrium is simply a state of the world where economic forces are balanced and in the absence of external influences the values of economic variables will not change. _____, for example, refers to a condition where a market price is established through competition such that the amount of goods or services sought by buyers is equal to the amount of goods or services produced by sellers
a. Market equilibrium28
b. Thing
c. Undefined
d. Undefined

29. In mathematics, _____ are the intuitive idea of a geometrical one-dimensional and continuous object.
a. Thing
b. Curves29
c. Undefined
d. Undefined

30. In economics, economic _____ is simply a state of the world where economic forces are balanced and in the absence of external influences the values of economic variables will not change.
a. Equilibrium30
b. Thing
c. Undefined
d. Undefined

31. In geometry, the _____ are a pair of special points used in describing conic sections. The four types of conic sections are the circle, parabola, ellipse, and hyperbola.

a. Foci31
b. Thing
c. Undefined
d. Undefined

32. In mathematics and in the sciences, a _____ is a concise way of expressing information symbolically or a general relationship between quantities.
   a. Thing
   b. Formula32
   c. Undefined
   d. Undefined

33. _____ is the distance around a given two-dimensional object. As a general rule, the _____ of a polygon can always be calculated by adding all the length of the sides together. So, the formula for triangles is P = a + b + c, where a, b and c stand for each side of it. For quadrilaterals the equation is P = a + b + c + d. For equilateral polygons, P = na, where n is the number of sides and a is the side length.
   a. Perimeter33
   b. Thing
   c. Undefined
   d. Undefined

34. In mathematics, the _____ is a conic section generated by the intersection of a right circular conical surface and a plane parallel to a generating straight line of that surface. It can also be defined as locus of points in a plane which are equidistant from a given point.
   a. Thing
   b. Parabola34
   c. Undefined
   d. Undefined

35. In philosophy, mathematics, and logic, a _____ is an attribute of an object; thus a red object is said to have the _____ of redness.
   a. Property35
   b. Thing
   c. Undefined
   d. Undefined

Chapter 7. Conic Sections and Non-Linear Systems

36. In astronomy, geography, geometry and related sciences and contexts, a plane is said to be _____ at a given point if it is locally perpendicular to the gradient of the gravity field, i.e., with the direction of the gravitational force at that point.
   a. Thing
   b. Horizontal36
   c. Undefined
   d. Undefined

37. In Euclidean geometry, an _____ is a closed segment of a differentiable curve in the two-dimensional plane; for example, a circular _____ is a segment of a circle.
   a. Arc37
   b. Concept
   c. Undefined
   d. Undefined

38. _____ also called rectification of a curve—was historically difficult.
   a. Thing
   b. Arc length38
   c. Undefined
   d. Undefined

39. _____ is the long dimension of any object. The _____ of a thing is the distance between its ends, its linear extent as measured from end to end.
   a. Thing
   b. Length39
   c. Undefined
   d. Undefined

40. In geometry, a line _____ is a part of a line that is bounded by two end points, and contains every point on the line between its end points.
   a. Segment40
   b. Concept
   c. Undefined
   d. Undefined

41. In physics, an _____ is the path that an object makes around another object while under the influence of a source of centripetal force, such as gravity.

a. Thing
b. Orbit41
c. Undefined
d. Undefined

42. _____ is a parameter associated with every conic section.
a. Eccentricity42
b. Thing
c. Undefined
d. Undefined

Chapter 8. Additional Topics in Algebra

1. In mathematics, a _____ is an ordered list of objects. Like a set, it contains members, also called elements or terms, and the number of terms is called the length of the _____. Unlike a set, order matters, and the exact same elements can appear multiple times at different positions in the _____.
   a. Sequence1
   b. Thing
   c. Undefined
   d. Undefined

2. In mathematics, a set is called _____ if there is a bijection between the set and some set of the form {1, 2, ..., n} where n is a natural number.
   a. Thing
   b. Finite2
   c. Undefined
   d. Undefined

3. A _____ is the sum of the elements of a sequence.
   a. Series3
   b. Thing
   c. Undefined
   d. Undefined

4. A _____ is any value or expression separated from another _____ by a + or - sign in an overall expression.
   a. Term4
   b. Thing
   c. Undefined
   d. Undefined

5. Leonardo of Pisa (1170s or 1180s – 1250), also known as Leonardo Pisano, Leonardo Bonacci, Leonardo _____, or, most commonly, simply _____, was an Italian mathematician, considered by some "the most talented mathematician of the Middle Ages."
   a. Person
   b. Fibonacci5
   c. Undefined
   d. Undefined

6. _____ is the state of being greater than any finite real or natural number, however large.

Chapter 8. Additional Topics in Algebra

   a. Thing
   b. Infinite6
   c. Undefined
   d. Undefined

7. _____ (1170s or 1180s – 1250), also known as Leonardo Pisano, Leonardo Bonacci, Leonardo Fibonacci, or, most commonly, simply Fibonacci, was an Italian mathematician, considered by some "the most talented mathematician of the Middle Ages."
   a. Person
   b. Leonardo of Pisa7
   c. Undefined
   d. Undefined

8. In mathematics, when a method of defining functions is utilized, in which the function being defined is applied within its own definition, that pertaining function is called _____.
   a. Thing
   b. Recursive8
   c. Undefined
   d. Undefined

9. _____ of a non-negative integer n is the product of all positive integers less than or equal to n.
   a. Factorial9
   b. Thing
   c. Undefined
   d. Undefined

10. Mathematical _____ is used in mathematics, and throughout the physical sciences, engineering, and economics. The complexity of such _____ ranges from relatively simple symbolic representations, such as numbers 1 and 2; function symbols sin and +, to conceptual symbols, such as lim and dy/dx; to equations and variables.
   a. Thing
   b. Notation10
   c. Undefined
   d. Undefined

11. A _____ is the result of the addition of a set of numbers. The numbers may be natural numbers, complex numbers, matrices, or still more complicated objects. An infinite _____ is a subtle procedure known as a series.

a. Sum11
b. Thing
c. Undefined
d. Undefined

12. _____ is the eighteenth letter of the Greek alphabet.
a. Sigma12
b. Thing
c. Undefined
d. Undefined

13. _____ is used as the symbol for summation. Summation is the addition of a set of numbers; the result is their sum. The "numbers" to be summed may be natural numbers, complex numbers, matrices, or still more complicated objects. An infinite sum is a subtle procedure known as a series.
a. Sigma notation13
b. Thing
c. Undefined
d. Undefined

14. _____ is the addition of a set of numbers; the result is their sum. The "numbers" to be summed may be natural numbers, complex numbers, matrices, or still more complicated objects. An infinite sum is a subtle procedure known as a series.
a. Summation14
b. Thing
c. Undefined
d. Undefined

15. A _____ typically refers to a class of handheld calculators that are capable of plotting graphs, solving equation systems, and performing numerous other tasks with variables.
a. Thing
b. Graphing calculator15
c. Undefined
d. Undefined

16. A _____ is a type of debt. All material things can be lent but this article focuses exclusively on monetary loans. Like all debt instruments, a _____ entails the redistribution of financial assets over time, between the lender and the borrower.
   a. Loan16
   b. Thing
   c. Undefined
   d. Undefined

17. _____ or arithmetics is the oldest and most elementary branch of mathematics, used by almost everyone, for tasks ranging from simple daily counting to advanced science and business calculations.
   a. Arithmetic17
   b. Thing
   c. Undefined
   d. Undefined

18. _____ is a sequence of numbers such that the difference of any two successive members of the sequence is a constant.
   a. Thing
   b. Arithmetic sequence18
   c. Undefined
   d. Undefined

19. _____ is one of the four basic arithmetic operations; it is essentially the opposite of addition.
   a. Thing
   b. Subtraction19
   c. Undefined
   d. Undefined

20. In mathematics, a _____ can mean either an element of the set {1, 2, 3, ...} (i.e the positive integers or the counting numbers) or an element of the set {0, 1, 2, 3, ...} (i.e. the non-negative integers).
   a. Thing
   b. Natural number20
   c. Undefined
   d. Undefined

Chapter 8. Additional Topics in Algebra

21. A _____ is a mathematical concept used to describe and assess quantity. It is an abstract entity representing a quantity, used to express how many are being referred to, or how much there is of some thing or property.
    a. Number21
    b. Thing
    c. Undefined
    d. Undefined

22. In plane geometry, a _____ is a polygon with four equal sides, four right angles, and parallel opposite sides. In algebra, the _____ of a number is that number multiplied by itself.
    a. Square22
    b. Thing
    c. Undefined
    d. Undefined

23. _____ is a part of mathematics concerned with questions of size, shape, and relative position of figures and with properties of space.
    a. Geometry23
    b. Thing
    c. Undefined
    d. Undefined

24. A _____ is a sequence of numbers where each term after the first is found by multiplying the previous one by a fixed non-zero number called the common ratio.
    a. Thing
    b. Geometric sequence24
    c. Undefined
    d. Undefined

25. A _____ is a quantity that denotes the proportional amount or magnitude of one quantity relative to another.
    a. Thing
    b. Ratio25
    c. Undefined
    d. Undefined

26. _____ is often represented as the sum of a sequence of terms.

a. Infinite series26
b. Thing
c. Undefined
d. Undefined

27. In geographic information systems, a _____ comprises an entity with a geographic location, typically determined by points, arcs, or polygons. Carriageways and cadastres exemplify _____ data.
   a. Thing
   b. Feature27
   c. Undefined
   d. Undefined

28. The mathematical concept of a _____ expresses the intuitive idea of deterministic dependence between two quantities, one of which is viewed as primary and the other as secondary. A _____ then is a way to associate a unique output for each input of a specified type, for example, a real number or an element of a given set.
   a. Function28
   b. Thing
   c. Undefined
   d. Undefined

29. In statistics, _____ means the most frequent value assumed by a random variable, or occurring in a sampling of a random variable.
   a. Mode29
   b. Concept
   c. Undefined
   d. Undefined

30. _____ are of a number n in its third power-the result of multiplying it by itself three times.
   a. Thing
   b. Cubes30
   c. Undefined
   d. Undefined

31. _____ is a method of mathematical proof typically used to establish that a given statement is true of all natural numbers

Chapter 8. Additional Topics in Algebra

a. Thing
b. Mathematical induction31
c. Undefined
d. Undefined

32. In arithmetic, the _____ refers to the number b in an expression of the form b^n.
   a. Base32
   b. Thing
   c. Undefined
   d. Undefined

33. A _____ consists either of a suggested explanation for a phenomenon or of a reasoned proposal suggesting a possible correlation between multiple phenomena.
   a. Thing
   b. Hypothesis33
   c. Undefined
   d. Undefined

34. In mathematics, for a statement to be mathematically _____, such a statement must be true of all natural numbers.
   a. Inductive34
   b. Thing
   c. Undefined
   d. Undefined

35. A _____ signifies a point or points of probability on a subject e.g., the _____ of creativity, which allows for the formation of rule or norm or law by interpretation of the phenomena events that can be created.
   a. Principle35
   b. Thing
   c. Undefined
   d. Undefined

36. _____ has many meanings, most of which simply .

a. Power36
b. Thing
c. Undefined
d. Undefined

37. In mathematics, an _____ number is a complex number whose square is a negative real number. They were defined in 1572 by Rafael Bombelli.
a. Thing
b. Imaginary37
c. Undefined
d. Undefined

38. In mathematics, the _____ i (or sometimes the Latin j or the Greek iota, see below) allows the real number system R to be extended to the complex number system C. Its precise definition is dependent upon the particular method of extension.
a. Thing
b. Imaginary unit38
c. Undefined
d. Undefined

39. A _____ is a simplified and structured visual representation of concepts, ideas, constructions, relations, statistical data, anatomy etc used in all aspects of human activities to visualize and clarify the topic.
a. Thing
b. Diagram39
c. Undefined
d. Undefined

40. In the scientific method, an _____ (Latin: ex-+-periri, "of (or from) trying"), is a set of actions and observations, performed in the context of solving a particular problem or question, in order to support or falsify a hypothesis or research concerning phenomena.
a. Thing
b. Experiment40
c. Undefined
d. Undefined

41. _____ is a subset of a population.

a. Thing
b. Sample41
c. Undefined
d. Undefined

42. In probability theory, the _____ or universal _____, often denoted S, Ù or U (for "universe"), of an experiment or random trial is the set of all possible outcomes.
    a. Sample space42
    b. Thing
    c. Undefined
    d. Undefined

43. _____ is a set, with some particular properties and usually some additional structure, such as the operations of addition or multiplication, for instance.
    a. Thing
    b. Space43
    c. Undefined
    d. Undefined

44. _____ is the mathematical action of repeatedly adding or subtracting one, usually to find out how many objects there are or to set aside a desired number of objects.
    a. Thing
    b. Counting44
    c. Undefined
    d. Undefined

45. _____ is the rearrangement of objects or symbols into distinguishable sequences.
    a. Permutation45
    b. Thing
    c. Undefined
    d. Undefined

46. In combinatorial mathematics, a _____ is an un-ordered collection of unique elements.

a. Combination46
b. Concept
c. Undefined
d. Undefined

47. In mathematics and in the sciences, a _____ is a concise way of expressing information symbolically or a general relationship between quantities.
a. Thing
b. Formula47
c. Undefined
d. Undefined

48. Blaise _____ was a French mathematician, physicist, and religious philosopher.
a. Pascal48
b. Person
c. Undefined
d. Undefined

49. _____ is the chance that something is likely to happen or be the case.
a. Thing
b. Probability49
c. Undefined
d. Undefined

50. _____ is a mathematical science pertaining to the collection, analysis, interpretation or explanation, and presentation of data. It is applicable to a wide variety of academic disciplines, from the physical and social sciences to the humanities.
a. Thing
b. Statistics50
c. Undefined
d. Undefined

51. In probability theory, _____ are various sets of outcomes (a subset of the sample space) to which a probability is assigned.

Chapter 8. Additional Topics in Algebra

a. Thing
b. Events51
c. Undefined
d. Undefined

52. A pair of angles are _____ if the sum of their angles is 90°.
a. Complementary52
b. Concept
c. Undefined
d. Undefined

53. In set theory and other branches of mathematics, two kinds of complements are defined, the relative _____ and the absolute _____.
a. Complement53
b. Thing
c. Undefined
d. Undefined

54. In logic, two _____ (or "mutual exclusive" according to some sources) propositions are propositions that logically cannot both be true.
a. Concept
b. Mutually exclusive54
c. Undefined
d. Undefined

55. In elementary algebra, a _____ is a polynomial with two terms: the sum of two monomials. It is the simplest kind of polynomial except for a monomial.
a. Binomial55
b. Thing
c. Undefined
d. Undefined

56. In mathematics, the _____ is an important formula giving the expansion of powers of sums.

Chapter 8. Additional Topics in Algebra

  a. Binomial theorem56
  b. Thing
  c. Undefined
  d. Undefined

57. _____ is a geometric arrangement of the binomial coefficients in a triangle. It is named after Blaise Pascal in the English-speaking world, even though others studied it centuries before him in Persia, China, India, and Italy.
  a. Thing
  b. Pascal's triangle57
  c. Undefined
  d. Undefined

58. In mathematics, a _____ is a statement that can be proved on the basis of explicitly stated or previously agreed assumptions.
  a. Thing
  b. Theorem58
  c. Undefined
  d. Undefined

59. A _____ is one of the basic shapes of geometry: a polygon with three vertices and three sides which are straight line segments.
  a. Triangle59
  b. Thing
  c. Undefined
  d. Undefined

60. In mathematics, particularly in combinatorics, the _____ of the natural number n and the integer k is the number of combinations that exist.
  a. Binomial coefficient60
  b. Thing
  c. Undefined
  d. Undefined

61. In mathematics, a _____ is a constant multiplicative factor of a certain object. The object can be such things as a variable, a vector, a function, etc. For example, the _____ of $9x^2$ is 9.

a. Thing
b. Coefficient61
c. Undefined
d. Undefined

62. An _____ of a product of sums expresses it as a sum of products by using the fact that multiplication distributes over addition.
a. Thing
b. Expansion62
c. Undefined
d. Undefined

63. _____ typically deals with the probability of several successive decisions, each of which has two possible outcomes.
a. Binomial probability63
b. Thing
c. Undefined
d. Undefined

64. _____ was a pre-Socratic Greek philosopher of southern Italy and a member of the Eleatic School founded by Parmenides.
a. Zeno of Elea64
b. Person
c. Undefined
d. Undefined

Chapter 1

1. b	2. a	3. b	4. a	5. a	6. b	7. a	8. a	9. b	10. b
11. a	12. a	13. a	14. b	15. b	16. a	17. a	18. a	19. a	20. b
21. a	22. a	23. b	24. b	25. b	26. b	27. a	28. b	29. b	30. b
31. a	32. a	33. a	34. a	35. a	36. a	37. a	38. b	39. b	40. a
41. b	42. a	43. b	44. b	45. b	46. a	47. a	48. b	49. a	50. b
51. a	52. b	53. b	54. a	55. b	56. b	57. b	58. a	59. a	60. b
61. a	62. a	63. b	64. b	65. a	66. b	67. a	68. b	69. a	70. b
71. a	72. a	73. a	74. a	75. b	76. b	77. b	78. b	79. b	80. a
81. b	82. a	83. b	84. b	85. a	86. b	87. b	88. b	89. b	90. b
91. b	92. a	93. b	94. a	95. a	96. b	97. b	98. a	99. b	100. a
101. a	102. b	103. b	104. b	105. a	106. a	107. b	108. a	109. a	110. b
111. b	112. b	113. b	114. b	115. a	116. a	117. a	118. b	119. a	120. b
121. b	122. b	123. a	124. a	125. a	126. a	127. a	128. b	129. b	130. b
131. a	132. b	133. b	134. b	135. a	136. a	137. a	138. a	139. a	140. b
141. a	142. a	143. b	144. b	145. b	146. b	147. b	148. b	149. b	150. a
151. a	152. a	153. a	154. a	155. b	156. a	157. a	158. b	159. a	160. a
161. a	162. a	163. a	164. b	165. a	166. a	167. b	168. a	169. b	170. a
171. a	172. a	173. a	174. a	175. b	176. b	177. b	178. b	179. a	180. b
181. b	182. a	183. b							

Chapter 2

1. a	2. b	3. b	4. a	5. a	6. b	7. b	8. a	9. a	10. a
11. a	12. b	13. b	14. b	15. a	16. b	17. b	18. b	19. b	20. b
21. a	22. a	23. b	24. b	25. a	26. a	27. a	28. a	29. b	30. a
31. b	32. b	33. b	34. b	35. b	36. a	37. a	38. a	39. a	40. b
41. a	42. b	43. a	44. b	45. a	46. b	47. a	48. b	49. b	50. b
51. a	52. a	53. a	54. b	55. a	56. b	57. a	58. b	59. b	60. a
61. a	62. a	63. b	64. b	65. b	66. a	67. a	68. b	69. b	70. a
71. b	72. b	73. b	74. b	75. a	76. b	77. a	78. b	79. b	80. b
81. b	82. b	83. a	84. b	85. b	86. b	87. b	88. b	89. b	90. a
91. a	92. b	93. b	94. a	95. a	96. b				

Chapter 3

1. a	2. a	3. a	4. a	5. a	6. b	7. b	8. a	9. b	10. b
11. a	12. a	13. a	14. a	15. a	16. b	17. b	18. a	19. a	20. a
21. b	22. b	23. a	24. a	25. a	26. b	27. a	28. b	29. b	30. a
31. b	32. a	33. a	34. b	35. b	36. b	37. b	38. a	39. a	40. b
41. b	42. b	43. b	44. b	45. a	46. b	47. a	48. a	49. a	50. a
51. b	52. a	53. a	54. b	55. a	56. a	57. a	58. b	59. a	60. a
61. a	62. b	63. b	64. b	65. a	66. a	67. b	68. b	69. b	70. b
71. b	72. b	73. a	74. b	75. b	76. b	77. b	78. a	79. b	80. b
81. a	82. b	83. b	84. a	85. b	86. a	87. a	88. b	89. a	90. b
91. a	92. a	93. a	94. b	95. a	96. b	97. b	98. b		

ANSWER KEY

Chapter 4

1. a	2. a	3. a	4. a	5. a	6. b	7. b	8. b	9. a	10. b
11. a	12. b	13. b	14. b	15. b	16. b	17. a	18. a	19. a	20. b
21. b	22. b	23. a	24. b	25. b	26. b	27. a	28. b	29. a	30. b
31. a	32. b	33. b	34. b	35. b	36. b	37. b	38. b	39. a	40. b
41. a	42. b	43. a	44. a	45. b	46. b	47. b	48. a	49. a	50. b
51. b	52. b	53. a	54. b	55. a	56. b	57. a	58. b	59. b	60. a
61. a	62. a	63. a	64. a	65. a	66. a	67. b	68. a	69. b	70. b

Chapter 5

1. a	2. b	3. a	4. b	5. a	6. a	7. a	8. b	9. a	10. a
11. a	12. b	13. b	14. a	15. a	16. b	17. b	18. a	19. a	20. b
21. b	22. b	23. a	24. b	25. a	26. b	27. a	28. b	29. b	30. b
31. a	32. b	33. b	34. a	35. a	36. a	37. a	38. b	39. b	40. b
41. b	42. a	43. b	44. b	45. b	46. b	47. a	48. b	49. a	50. a
51. a	52. a	53. b	54. a	55. b	56. a	57. a	58. b	59. a	60. b
61. b	62. a	63. b	64. a						

Chapter 6

1. b	2. b	3. b	4. a	5. b	6. a	7. b	8. a	9. a	10. b
11. a	12. b	13. b	14. a	15. a	16. a	17. b	18. a	19. b	20. a
21. b	22. a	23. a	24. b	25. b	26. a	27. b	28. a	29. a	30. b
31. a	32. b	33. a	34. b	35. a	36. b	37. b	38. b	39. b	40. a
41. a	42. b	43. b	44. b	45. a	46. b	47. a	48. a	49. b	50. b
51. b	52. b	53. b	54. b	55. b	56. a	57. a	58. b	59. b	60. b
61. b	62. b	63. a	64. a	65. b	66. a	67. b	68. a	69. a	70. b
71. a	72. b	73. b	74. b	75. a	76. a	77. a	78. b	79. a	80. a
81. a	82. b	83. a							

Chapter 7

1. a	2. a	3. b	4. b	5. a	6. a	7. b	8. a	9. b	10. b
11. a	12. a	13. a	14. a	15. a	16. a	17. a	18. a	19. a	20. b
21. b	22. b	23. b	24. a	25. a	26. a	27. a	28. a	29. b	30. a
31. a	32. b	33. a	34. b	35. a	36. b	37. a	38. b	39. b	40. a
41. b	42. a								

Chapter 8

1. a	2. b	3. a	4. a	5. b	6. b	7. b	8. b	9. a	10. b
11. a	12. a	13. a	14. a	15. b	16. a	17. a	18. b	19. b	20. b
21. a	22. a	23. a	24. b	25. b	26. a	27. b	28. a	29. a	30. b
31. b	32. a	33. b	34. a	35. a	36. a	37. b	38. b	39. b	40. b
41. b	42. a	43. b	44. b	45. a	46. a	47. b	48. a	49. b	50. b
51. b	52. a	53. a	54. b	55. a	56. b	57. b	58. b	59. a	60. a
61. b	62. b	63. a	64. a						